PART I:
EQUIPPING YOURSELF

To Tina with love

Contents

✦

Introduction

Albert Einstein once said, "Imagination is more important than knowledge. It enlarges your vision, stretches the mind, challenges the impossible." He probably wasn't thinking specifically of amateur astronomy, but he could have been. The specks of light we see in the sky at night are the biggest, hottest, farthest, fastest, oldest, and grandest objects in the entire universe. Yet we can go outside and see them for ourselves. The lure of the sky is that we see with our own eyes the most spectacular objects in the universe. Imagination is important because these distant objects appear so small and so faint that we have to interpret what we are seeing. Without interpretation, they remain specks. Our imagination turns a pair of faint glimmers visible only through a telescope into two giant stars, each a hundred times the size of our sun, separated by a thousand times the distance from the earth to the sun, and so distant that it took light two hundred years to travel from them to our eye; then we are humbled and impressed. Hundreds of such objects lurk in the sky, and this book interprets them so your imagination can stretch your mind.

This book is a guide to the wonders of the sky for beginning amateur astronomers who, with binoculars or small telescopes, want to observe the sky. It highlights and interprets almost two hundred of the brightest and most accessible multiple stars, star clusters, nebulae, and galaxies. Use this book in conjunction with a modest star atlas (see list on pp. 91–92) to begin a rewarding hobby of serious stargazing.

Use it also to gain a deeper appreciation for wonders closer to home: the sun, moon, planets, comets, and meteors. The moon can seem so familiar that one can easily believe there is nothing new about it of interest to see. This book shows that, in fact, there is more than meets the eye if the eye knows what to look for. This is especially true for eclipses, where, to the initiated, a wonderful panorama unfolds.

In addition, the book offers tips on how to select basic equipment, how to observe, and where to go for further information. It is your guide to getting started in amateur astronomy and to knowing how to "read" the sky.

A tourist visiting a foreign city wants to know how to get the most out of his or her stay. Like a guide to the hotels and sights of a vacation destination, this book advises you what to see and do when you arrive at your telescopic target.

✦

Chapter One

SELECTING BINOCULARS, TELESCOPES, AND ACCESSORIES

You can see a lot with only your eyes, especially if you know what to look for, and naked-eye stargazing is an underappreciated art. Your eyes take in wide areas of the sky, allowing you to see several constellations at once to observe how they relate to one another. Faint objects within constellations, however, such as galaxies and star clusters, require binoculars or a telescope, and sooner or later (usually sooner), all amateur astronomers want a telescope. Because telescopes gather more light than the eye does, they make faint things bright and magnify them, revealing structure and detail.

The best beginner's telescope is often a pair of binoculars, especially if the budget is limited. A pair of binoculars is actually a pair of small telescopes operating in tandem. The best astronomy binoculars are labeled 7 × 50 or, preferably, 10 × 50. Such binoculars magnify seven or ten times and have a front lens diameter of 50 millimeters. A large lens is not essential for sporting events, where 35mm might suffice, but it is critical in astronomy, where the whole idea is to gather as much light as possible. Smaller binoculars, such as 7 × 35s or 6 × 24s, have smaller front lenses and do not gather enough light to show faint stars. The front lenses of a pair of 7 × 50 binoculars collect twice as much light as 7 × 35 binoculars do. Larger or higher-power binoculars, such as 11 × 80s, are expensive and need a tripod, although they give excellent views of the sky. If you wear glasses, test the binoculars you propose to purchase to ensure they will focus to infinity with your glasses off; you definitely do not want to wear glasses while looking through lenses (binocular or telescope). Be sure the binoculars have center focus (both sides focus simultaneously) and avoid focus-free binoculars (which don't focus well at all). The best binoculars can be found at camera and telescope stores. Avoid the cheapest binoculars at discount stores (especially those made of plastic), and ask about lens antireflection coatings. Multiple coatings improve the contrast—an important plus for nighttime observing. Expect to pay no less than $100 for a good pair that will last a lifetime.

Binoculars have the advantage of portability. They are easy to take along on summer vacations to national parks and other dark places away from urban lights, when a telescope would likely be left at home. Also, binoculars are excellent for exploring the Milky Way. With binoculars, you will see more structure in our Milky Way than in all the deep space objects put together as seen through a large telescope. Binoculars too will be useful in scouting out faint objects you are trying to locate with a telescope. Even if you own a very large telescope, you will enjoy using binoculars for unparalleled wide views of the sky.

One step up from binoculars is a spotting telescope. Relatively inexpensive and portable, a low-power spotting telescope mounted on a camera tripod gives superb wide-angle views of the Milky Way as well as of the brighter nebulae and star clusters. Most of the interesting objects in the constellations identified in this book are visible with a spotting scope. A spotting scope can be operated at much higher power than can binoculars (perhaps as high as 100×), and it will let you "zoom in" on the planets and other small objects. Spotting scopes are sold in gun stores, sporting goods shops, and camera stores. Prices range from less than $100 to well over $1,000. Many amateur astronomers who own large (and nonportable) telescopes keep a spotting scope handy for traveling as well as for bright, wide-angle views of the Milky Way. As is true for binoculars, you get what you pay for, and a good spotting telescope will last a lifetime.

Eventually, all astronomy buffs want a big telescope. The larger the telescope's diameter, the more light it gathers and the brighter it makes faint objects appear; a large telescope will show more faint objects and show them better than a small telescope will. A telescope also magnifies the object under inspection, but the amount of magnification (or "power") is less important than most people think. The distortion created by heat currents in our atmosphere limits the amount you can magnify a planet or galaxy, and experienced observers generally use surprisingly low magnifications. Even a large telescope seldom gains by using magnifications greater than 200 or so times, and such power is useful on few objects and then only when the earth's atmosphere is unusually steady. Hint: If you

✦ TELESCOPE POWER ✦

The magnification of a telescope comes from the combined optics of the main lens or mirror and the eyepiece. Each lens, mirror, and eyepiece has its own focal length— the distance it takes to bring light to a focus. To find the magnification of a telescope when used with a specific eyepiece, divide the focal length of the telescope by the focal length of the eyepiece. For example, a telescope with a focal length of 800mm used with a 20mm eyepiece will have a magnification of 40. The same telescope used with a 10mm eyepiece will have a magnification of 80. You change the magnification of a telescope by changing the eyepiece, but each telescope is capable of only a set range of magnifications. Any telescope can be made to magnify as much as you want, but after a point the quality of the image suffers unbearably. Most amateurs use low magnifications most of the time and save high powers for rare occasions of unusual atmospheric stability.

The ability of a telescope to see faint objects depends on the area of its main lens or mirror. To compare the light-gathering ability of two telescopes, remember that the areas of two circles are proportional to the squares of their diameters (the diameter times itself). A 6-inch mirror collects ½ as much light as does an 8-inch (36 v. 64) and only one-third as much as does a 10-inch mirror (36 v. 100).

The power of a telescope ("power" meaning the ability to shows things well, rather than show them big) depends largely on the size of the mirror, all other things being equal.

see a telescope advertised on the basis of its magnification ("454-power telescope!"), stay away from it. In practice, low magnification gives sharper and wider images than does high magnification.

The amount of light a telescope gathers depends solely on the diameter of its mirror or lens. All other things being equal, the larger the better—but all other things are seldom equal. A 6-inch-diameter telescope is a great starter telescope that is sure to reveal marvelous things.

Often overlooked by novices is the design and sturdiness of the telescope's mounting. A flimsy and under-designed telescope, like the kind often seen in department stores, is frustrating to use. It is difficult to aim a telescope that lacks a solid mounting, and it is even more difficult as the earth rotates to track an object under high magnification. All too often, first-time buyers purchase a telescope based on its claimed "power" while over-looking its wobbly mounting, only to discover they bought a bundle of frustration and an instrument that will probably sit in the garage. The mount should be sturdy enough to let you move the scope smoothly and to make tiny adjustments to its position.

In addition to quality of construction, the design of the mounting is important. *Equatorial* mounts let you easily track an object as the earth rotates by slewing the telescope on only one axis. This is far easier than trying to turn the telescope on two axes simultaneously. Equatorial mounts can also be motorized to track objects automatically and keep them continuously in view within the eyepiece.

Telescopes come in several styles. The most popular are refractors, Newtonian reflectors (which are commonly equipped with equatorial or Dobsonian mountings), and Schmidt-Cassegrain reflectors. Naturally, each has its advantages and disadvantages; there is no "best" telescope.

Refracting telescopes use a lens to focus light by "refracting" or bending it to a point. It is time consuming to grind the multiple surfaces of a lens properly, and refracting telescopes over about 4 inches in diameter are expensive (but generally of high quality). Most sold through mass markets are much smaller. The typical department or toy store telescope is a refractor with a lens 60 to 90mm (2 to 3 inches) in diameter. In general,

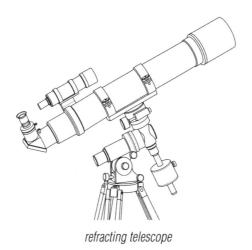

refracting telescope

these small telescopes, often advertised as good starter telescopes for kids, perform like the toys they are and are more likely to bring frustration than joy. Such $249 "494 power!" toys lack the stability and optical quality needed to reveal the wonders of the heavens, and the money is much better spent on a pair of binoculars or a spotting telescope or saved for a real telescope. Much more expensive refractors over 3 inches in diameter and costing well over $1,000 are excellent telescopes; they are sold mainly in telescope stores and some camera shops. Because of their generally sharp images, refractors are favored by people who study the planets, but their relatively small sizes (dollar for dollar) make them a poorer choice for people interested in faint star clusters and galaxies.

Newtonian reflectors use a mirror to concentrate light and send it to the eyepiece, which is positioned on the side of a long tube. Simple in design, they are relatively inexpensive for their size. Most of the small Newtonian reflectors in the 3- and 4-inch size range found in department and toy stores for under $300 should be avoided. Newtonian reflectors 6 inches and larger with an *equatorial mount* are another matter. Generally costing $400 and up, they used to be the workhorses of amateur astronomers. They gather a lot of light for their cost and show more faint star clusters and galaxies than a person could see in years of hunting. Also, they tolerate high magnification and show the planets surprisingly well. The popular equatorial mount has one axis that parallels the axis of the earth and another perpendicular to it, a real advantage in tracking objects as the earth turns. A motorized drive makes this kind of telescope even more convenient when using high power. The image formed is clear enough to justify the additional expense of good eyepieces. The main disadvantage of these telescopes is their bulk. All in all, a properly made 6- or 8-inch is a great starter telescope that will give a lifetime of service.

Newtonian reflecting telescope on equatorial mount

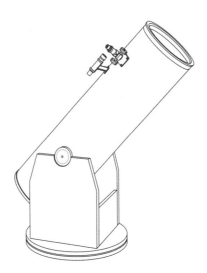

Dobsonian reflecting telescope

Newtonian reflectors with the type of simple mounting invented by John Dobson are popular in larger sizes, where an equatorial mount would be prohibitively expensive and cumbersome. Rather than sitting atop a tripod or pier with a complex equatorial mechanism, a *Dobsonian* telescope is cradled in a box supported by Teflon bearings. The disadvantage is a lack of equatorial mounting (which precludes time-exposure photography); the advantage is low cost and simplicity of operation. A complete 6-inch Dobsonian telescope can be found for under $400 and an 8-inch for about $500. It's no surprise that this kind of telescope is so popular. A 6- or 8-inch Dobsonian is highly recommended as an excellent first telescope for a child or adult. Look for one in telescope stores and mail-order catalogs. Virtually all giant amateur telescopes with mirrors 16 inches in diameter or larger (unheard of until a few years ago) are Dobsonian in design. Some are computer controlled and quite sophisticated.

Both Newtonian and Dobsonian reflectors need to be adjusted frequently to keep the optics in alignment. While not difficult, this requires more of the owner than does a refractor or Schmidt-Cassegrain.

Schmidt-Cassegrains combine a mirror and correcting lens to produce in a smaller package the equivalent of a Newtonian reflector image. While an 8-inch Newtonian reflector won't fit in the trunk of a small car, you can store an 8-inch Schmidt-Cassegrain (plus the tripod) in a box the size of a large suitcase. This sophisticated and generally well-made instrument is the telescope of choice where portability is important or storage space is at a premium. The 16-inch Smith-Cassegrain is a small observatory telescope. It generally comes with an equatorial mount, motorized drive, and slow-motion controls. The

Schmidt-Cassegrain telescope

(Large manufacturers produce a variety of sizes and types of telescopes and accessories, which are sold through camera, electronics, and telescope stores and by mail. Check a current astronomy magazine for advertisements.)

trade-off is cost; a Schmidt-Cassegrain costs more than twice as much as a Newtonian reflector of the same diameter and ability and perhaps three times as much as an equivalent Dobsonian. The fanciest Schmidt-Cassegrain telescopes are outfitted with computer controls and even electronic cameras.

Nothing will improve the quality of a telescope more than a good set of eyepieces. The telescope's main lens or mirror might form a clear, bright image, but it depends on the eyepiece to display that image properly. A cheap eyepiece displays a poorly focused image in a narrow angle of view; an excellent eyepiece shows sharp images with high contrast in a much more pleasing wide-angle view. An analogy would be using cheap speakers with a high-quality stereo system. Good eyepieces are surprisingly expensive. Because most telescopes come with inexpensive eyepieces as accessories, it is best to bite the bullet and figure in the cost of replacing them—or at least adding to them—as part of the initial cost of the telescope. The best eyepieces cost over $200 each, but adequate ones can be found for considerably less. A set of three for low, medium, and high power is all a person needs.

Other accessories include a small "finder telescope" attached to the main telescope and useful for locating objects (the Telrad type is very popular), carrying cases, a lens cleaning kit, flashlight with red filter, case for carrying reference books and star charts, and perhaps a small tool kit.

Some people enjoy photographing the sky. Photographing planets and galaxies, which takes specialized and expensive equipment and lots of experience, is amazingly difficult. It is easy, however, to photograph the constellations and the Milky Way. For constellation photography you need only a camera that will let you take time

✦ EYEPIECES ✦

Eyepieces are miniature telescopes that magnify and display the image created by the telescope's main lens or mirror. They come in a variety of sizes, measured in millimeters. A 25- to 40mm eyepiece provides very low-power wide-angle views of the sky. It is easy to find things with a low-power eyepiece and to keep objects in view as the earth turns. Use low-power eyepieces on extended deep-space objects such as nebulae and star clusters.

Medium-power eyepieces (10 to 20mm) are better for the moon and planets and for small deep-space objects that require some magnification.

High-power eyepieces (9mm and smaller) are effective only when the air is exceptionally steady, which might not be often. When conditions permit, use high power on planets, close double stars, and some deep-space objects. Keep in mind that with high power, the field of view is proportionately narrow and the ability to find and track is relatively limited.

Barlow lenses are "helper eyepieces" that double or triple the power of an existing eyepiece. They are relatively inexpensive, and a Barlow used with a low-power eyepiece serves as a perfectly adequate medium-power eyepiece.

Avoid telescopes that come with 0.96-inch (24mm) eyepieces, as they are invariably inferior in construction.

The major mistake beginners make is trying to use too high a magnification.

exposures, a cable release, and a tripod. Use fast film, and take exposures from 30 seconds to 10 minutes in duration using different lenses. Unless your tripod is motorized to compensate for the earth's rotation, the star images will become short streaks after a few minutes (you can take longer exposures before the stars begin to streak with a wide-angle lens). Keep notes on the circumstances of each exposure so you know what worked and what did not, and experiment to find the settings that work best for you. Include foreground trees and hills (and even people), especially when in a scenic vacation setting. CCD astrophotography, which uses electronic cameras with Charged Couple Devices rather than film, is becoming increasingly popular. Be aware, however, that it requires top-of-the-line equipment, a portable computer, and substantial experience.

The best advice for selecting a first telescope is to avoid toy and department stores. Read the advertisements in astronomy magazines and send for promotional literature to become familiar with the range of what is available. Visit camera and electronics stores that carry telescopes, but look past the small refractors and reflectors. Buy binoculars or a spotting scope if your budget is under $300. Consider a Dobsonian or Newtonian reflector 6 inches or larger, and budget for replacement eyepieces. Planetariums and especially astronomy clubs can offer the kind of honest advice a customer is less likely to get from a salesman or from manufacturers' brochures.

Chapter Two

✧

TIPS ON OBSERVING THE SKY

It might sound silly to ask how to observe the sky. Don't you just go outside at night and look up? There's a bit more to it than that. First, it is far better to observe from a dark place. You will see *many* more stars if the sky is dark. If you live in a city, there's not much you can do about its millions of lights, but you can make sure that the lights around your house are turned off. Also, find an observing place away from trees and street lights.

For many people, the best time to observe the stars is while on vacation, especially when visiting national parks and other remote areas where it is astoundingly dark at night. Many amateur astronomers occasionally escape to locations outside the city for the best views of deep-space objects, and local astronomy clubs have permanent observing sites where they gather in the dark of the moon for "star parties." Remember that bright moonlight the week before and after the full moon turns even the darkest sky into perpetual twilight.

Needless to say, if you're not comfortable, you won't enjoy sky gazing. Remember that the temperature drops during the night, and even a chilly evening can become a cold night. Experienced skywatchers know to dress warmly. Hats are important in cold weather. Your body generates less heat if you're standing around stargazing than if you're moving around, as football fans know well. Thick insulated boots are another must in cold weather.

Give your eyes time to adjust to the darkness. When you step outside from a brightly lit room, you cannot see much at first. Allow several minutes for your eyes to develop "night vision." Then avoid overly bright lights while you observe. Astronomers use a red flash-light to read notes and star charts, as red light does not affect night vision as much as white light does. To provide yourself a dim red light to read by, place a piece of red cellophane over the lens of a small penlight. Headlights are a major "no-no" at star parties.

Telescopes are particularly sensitive to changes in temperature during cool weather. The optics (especially the main lens or mirror) work best at the outside ambient temper-ature. While cooling from a warm room or garage, the optics change shape and perform poorly until they have thermally stabilized. This is true even in professional observatories, which reduce the effect by refrigerating the telescope during the day to the anticipated nighttime temperature. No, we cannot store our telescopes in the refrigerator, but we can store them in the coolest place compatible with safety and cleanliness, or we can take them outside and let them cool down an hour or more before beginning to observe. When it is not possible to precool a telescope in the winter, be prepared to lose the first hour of observing while the telescope reaches thermal equilibrium.

Telescopes are also surprisingly sensitive to air currents. You have seen air rising from the asphalt of a parking lot on a hot day; a telescope magnifies air currents just as it mag-nifies stars, and even minor drafts of warm air that you might not otherwise notice will wreck the clarity of an image. Therefore, avoid observing from pavement, which, when warmed during the day, retains heat for several hours after sunset, and do not observe atop warm buildings (observe instead from a grassy or dirt area). Even your own body heat can seriously interfere on a cool night. Stand so that any breeze will carry the heat from your body away from the telescope, and keep warm objects away from the telescope, too.

Another problem is dew. Moisture likes to condense on cool surfaces, especially lenses. Except in the ultradry desert, as the temperature drops, your telescope will collect moisture. Tubes that project beyond your main lens can prevent dew from collecting and ending your night of observing; some people use gentle heaters or even hair dryers. You can lessen the problem by not breathing on your eyepieces or finder telescope.

Lastly, take time to see. Other than the sun and moon, astronomical objects are faint and distant and their features subtle. You will see little at first glance. Take time to tease out the detail. Faint and delicate markings will appear only gradually. The great astronomer William Herschel, discoverer of the planet Uranus and one of the greatest observers of all time, said, "You must not expect to see 'at sight.' Seeing is in some respects an art which must be learned. Many a night have I been practicing to see, and it would be strange if one did not acquire a certain dexterity by such constant practice." Have patience, and take time to see.

PART II:
THE SOLAR SYSTEM

Chapter Three

∗

OBSERVING THE SUN

The sun is so obvious it is often neglected. Still, it remains as interesting as it is accessible. It is the only star in the sky whose surface we can see, and (except near sunspot minimum, when it is featureless) the sun's face changes daily.

Of course, you must never look directly at the sun with or without a telescope. The sun's light is so intense it can cause permanent eye damage faster than you can react, and the eye has no pain sensors to warn of disaster. Observe the sun only with a properly filtered telescope. Use a sun filter or project the sun's image. Do *not* make your own sun filter; the sun may *look* properly filtered, but its infrared and ultraviolet light—which your eye cannot see and your filter may not block—are strong enough to cause immediate and permanent damage. Use only commercially available solar filters purchased from a reputable source. Welder's #14 filters are safe and inexpensive but can be difficult to find.

Special sun filters made of dark glass or plastic, aluminized glass or plastic, or aluminized mylar are available at many telescope stores and planetarium gift shops. A dark filter absorbs sunlight while aluminized filters allow only a small fraction to pass through. Aluminized glass gives the best performance but is expensive; aluminized mylar is effective and inexpensive but easily torn.

Never put a filter at the *eyepiece* end of a telescope. Once sunlight has become concentrated, it is too hot for a filter to absorb. The filter will likely crack—possibly while you are looking through it. A filter must fit over the *front end* of the telescope so it reduces the sun's intensity *before* entering the eyepiece. If your telescope came equipped with a solar filter that screws into the eyepiece, discard it.

The other common technique for observing the sun is to project its image with a telescope or binoculars onto a shaded white projection screen. The magnified image is quite bright and can be viewed by several people at a time (such as a school class), making it easy to point out features to others. You can photograph the sun's features in detail if you set your camera to overexpose the image. A word of caution—do *not* use good binoculars or an expensive multiple-lens telescope eyepiece. The sun's concentrated heat can crack or unglue an eyepiece! Do not risk using equipment you cannot afford to lose. Because the sun's heat builds up inside a Schmidt-Cassegrain telescope, such closed-tube telescopes should be pointed at the sun for only a few minutes at a time and then turned away and allowed to cool. Cover most of the front lens of a large telescope and let light pass through a small hole no more than 3 inches in diameter.

Without a telescope you will see only the rare naked-eye sunspot. Through a properly filtered telescope, however, there is much to see. Sunspots—cooler and darker areas of the sun's surface—may dot the sun's face. The smallest sunspots are the size of the moon and the largest are a hundred times the size of the earth! Notice that sunspots have complex structures and often come in pairs or groups. Sunspots have a dark inner umbra and lighter outer penumbra, which may show the effect of magnetic fields. Large spots, which have quite an intricate structure, are often connected to their neighbors. Notice that spots near the edge of the sun are foreshortened by the angle of view.

Sunspots live for days or weeks and change in unpredictable ways. Since the sun rotates in less than a month, you can watch sunspots grow, evolve, and fade as they slowly march across the sun's rotating face. Large spots and groups change noticeably in the span of just a few hours. You can follow a spot through its life cycle to witness change in the sky where at first glance there might seem to have been none.

For a long-term amateur project, count the number of spots visible on the sun's surface during several years (or decades) to monitor the 11-year sunspot cycle. The sun's activity waxes and wanes in a cycle with a period that averages 11 years. The peak near the turn of the millennium will be followed by a decline until the next peak around or soon after the year 2010. At sunspot minimum, few or no spots appear, while at maximum the sun's face is spotted every day. Counting spots involves more than merely adding up their number. To determine the Relative Sunspot Number, multiply the number of sunspot groups by 10, and then add the number of individual spots. Two sunspot groups of four spots each plus three individual spots yield a RSN of 31 ($2 \times 10 + 8 + 3 = 31$).

Flares—abrupt explosive events on the sun's surface—are reported in the news when they disrupt the earth's magnetic field and disturb its ionosphere and electric power grid, but only the very brightest can be seen without highly specialized equipment. When visible, they look like brief brightenings in the sun's surface. They cannot be predicted in advance.

Prominences—the "flames" seen silhouetted against the sky around the edge of the sun—also require special equipment, costing well over $1,000. Prominences are so much fainter than the disk of the sun they can be seen only with narrow-wavelength filters that eliminate most of the sun's light. They can also be seen during a total solar eclipse.

Chapter Four

✦

OBSERVING THE MOON

The moon, the second brightest object in the sky, is perhaps the most rewarding to observe. You can follow its motions and phases with your eyes alone, and even a small telescope will show wonderful detail. Plus the moon is visible half the time.

THE MOON'S MOTION

The most obvious aspect of the moon is its changing phase. One side is illuminated by the sun while the other side is in darkness (this is true for any globe in full sunlight), but these shift in a monthly cycle as the moon orbits the earth. The cycle of the moon's phases was probably the first astronomical cycle to be noticed many thousands of years ago, yet it continues to confuse people today. A complication is that the moon keeps one face permanently turned toward the earth. How does the angle of sunlight change on the moon through the month while the moon keeps one face toward the earth? This simple analogy may help.

Place a chair on the lawn in the sun. Imagine that the sun is low in the sky. The chair represents the earth; you are the moon, and the sun remains the sun. Step counterclockwise in a large circle around the chair, always facing it, and notice what happens to the sunlight on your head. At one point in your orbit you are facing the chair while the sun is behind you; the back of your head is illuminated and your face is dark. A person sitting in the chair would see no light on your face; you are at "new moon" (which equals "no moon" as seen from the chair/earth). After a few steps to the right, the left part of your

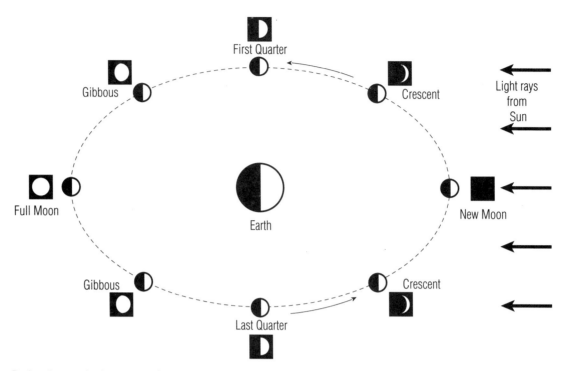

During the month, the moon makes a complete circuit of the sky. Our calendar month approximates the lunar month, and our week approximates a quarter of a month.

face becomes illuminated and a person in the chair sees a crescent of light on your face. One quarter of an orbit after "new," the left half of your face is lit while the other half is dark. Your face is half-lit, but you are at "first quarter" because you have traveled the first quarter of the way around the earth. Another quarter of an orbit later and you will be facing both the chair and the sun; your face is fully illuminated and a person sitting in the chair will see a "full moon." One quarter of an orbit later the sun will shine on the right side of your face. You now appear as a half-moon, but you are at "three-quarters" phase because you have gone three-quarters of the way around the chair/earth. After a final quarter orbit you have returned to "new." One lunar cycle takes just over 29 days, or one lunar month.

As interesting as the moon is, astronomers despise its light. Between the first and last quarter, and especially for the few days around the full moon, the moon's light turns beautiful dark country skies into pale, citylike canopies. Fainter, deep-space objects so beloved by amateur and professional astronomers alike are then lost to sight. The only recourse is to abandon observing all but the moon and planets for those days each month when the moon's light overwhelms all else.

LUNAR OCCULTATIONS

The moon's motion around the earth carries it through the sky and the sky's background of stars. The moon frequently passes near a planet or star; more rarely it eclipses (or occults, to use the more correct term) a distant object. Occultations of planets and bright stars occur up to several times a year from a given location, and their rarity makes them a novelty that should not be missed. When the moon occults a star, the star blinks out in a fraction of a second in a case of now-you-see-it, now-you-don't. A planet takes up to a minute to disappear behind the moon's disk. Up to an hour or so later, the star or planet reappears as the moon moves on. Because the moon is so much brighter than the star or planet, binoculars or a telescope are a must for viewing occultations. Upcoming occultations are noted in annual publications like the Royal Astronomical Society of Canada's *Observer's Handbook* and in monthly sky columns in popular astronomy magazines.

THE MOON THROUGH A TELESCOPE

The moon's phases can be seen by anyone, but if you have a telescope, you can enjoy its myriad surface features. The moon is one of the most rewarding telescopic objects. It is so near and so large that even the smallest telescope will show a surprising number of features. In fact, a huge telescope does not show significantly more than a small one. Anyone who looks at the moon for the first time through any size telescope is impressed.

Nothing on the moon gives you a feel for the scale of what you are seeing. Even knowing that it is 2,000 miles in diameter fails to put things into perspective. Visualize the craters Copernicus and Tycho, which are more than 50 miles across, or Mare Imbrium, which is twice the size of Texas, superimposed on your state map to appreciate the scale of the moon's features.

The appearance of the moon changes dramatically as the month passes because the lighting angle changes. Landscape photographers know that the best time to photograph scenery is early in the morning or late in the afternoon when the sun angle is low and shadows are present, whereas during the middle of the day the landscape seems "flat" and without contrast. This is even more so on the moon. There, because everything is essentially the same gray color, only shadows reveal the topography. The boundary between the lit side of the moon and its dark side is the *terminator*. A constantly moving line that runs from near the moon's north pole to its south pole, the terminator marks the points where the sun is rising or setting. Between new and full moons, the terminator we see marks the sunrise line, and between the full moon and the following new moon, the terminator viewed marks the sunset line. The terminator moves across almost ⅓₀th the face of the moon each day, and each night it appears 12 degrees from where it was the night before. Follow the terminator during the lunar month and watch it reveal a changing procession of craters, seas, and mountains. Each feature is clearly visible for only a few days before the sun is high, thereby dispelling shadows and "flattening" it. No feature appears the same two nights in a row. The worst time to moon gaze is during the full moon because shadows are totally absent then (although at full moon, the white rays that radiate from major craters show up best).

The moon is covered with *craters*. These formed when comets and asteroids slammed into the surface and exploded. While neither comets nor asteroids are made of explosive material, even an inert chunk of ice or rock explodes when it is traveling at hypersonic speeds and then suddenly stops. The object's energy of motion is abruptly changed into heat, and enough heat is generated to vaporize the impacting object, along with a great deal of whatever it hits; an object the size of a large house traveling at 100,000 miles per hour creates a crater a mile across. That is how craters form on all the planets and moons. Although the earth has craters, erosion soon erases them, while on the airless moon, they remain fresh for hundreds of millions, or even billions, of years.

Perhaps the most beautiful of the moon's craters is Copernicus. It is also one of the moon's youngest major craters, having formed "only" 900 million years ago. Its walls are as high as the Rocky Mountains. Copernicus's *rays*, which consist of pulverized rock debris violently thrown outward during the impact, are conspicuous when the sun angle is high, near full moon. Notice the chains of smaller secondary craters around Copernicus, which formed immediately following the impact when large chunks of debris fell back to the moon and exploded.

Most craters appear in the lunar *highlands*. The highlands are the oldest part of the moon's surface. There, asteroids of various sizes slammed into the surface, exploded, and blasted out countless craters during a period of intense bombardment lasting the first few hundred million years of the moon's history and leaving no square inch of the moon's surface untouched. About 300,000 craters are visible from the earth. The smallest craters we see are about a half-mile across—almost the size of the famous Meteor Crater in Arizona. Relatively few new craters form today.

The largest impact structures are called *basins*. They are "supercraters," with more than one concentric outer wall. The Imbrium Basin, the most conspicuous basin to us (a larger one is located on the moon's far side), is twice the size of Texas. It was created almost 4 billion years ago when an asteroid a hundred miles across struck the moon's

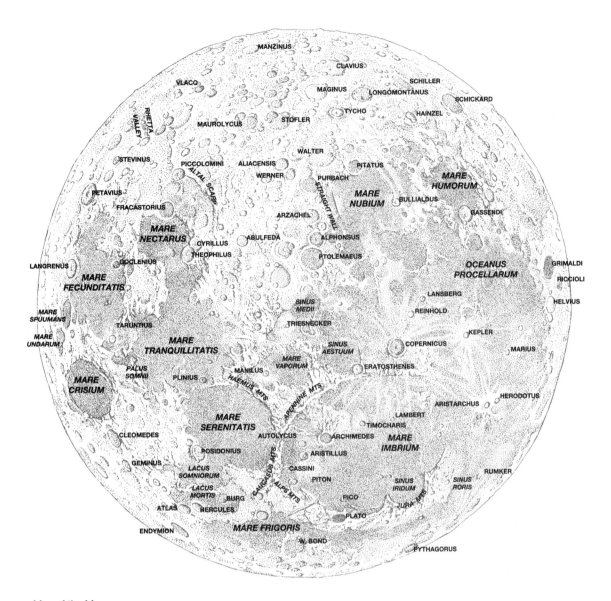

Map of the Moon

surface with the force of 750 billion atomic bombs. The mountains ringing the Imbrium Basin and other basins are actually the walls of huge impact craters.

The moon's darker areas are called *seas* (or *maria*, which is Latin for seas). Darkness on the moon is a matter of degree; the light areas reflect about 10 percent of the light that hits them and the dark areas only 5 percent, so in reality the entire surface of the moon is quite dark. The seas cover ⅓ of the near side of the moon.

The seas are vast dark lava plains, marking where lava seeped up from below the moon's surface and flooded its low-lying areas more than 3 billion years ago. The last lava flow cooled more than 3 billion years ago. Previously, the entire surface of the moon appeared heavily cratered, like the highlands. You see few craters on the seas, because few asteroids and comets have fallen since the moon cooled and lava stopped flowing, smoothing out its lowlands.

There is so much to look at on the moon. The seas and major craters are easily identified, and it is fun to watch their appearance change as shadows advance and recede during the lunar month. There are also less conspicuous objects to marvel at once you locate them, such as the sinuous *rilles*. Rilles, which crisscross the seas, are collapsed lava tubes. Wrinkled *ridges* on the seas mark where lava piled up high; look for ridges at very low sun angles. Among the more curious features are the Alpine Valley, an 80-mile-long gash on the northwest edge of Mare Imbrium, and the Straight Wall, a 70-mile-long 800-foot-high slope (not cliff) in Mare Nubium. As is so often the case, the more you look, the more you see. There is more on the moon than you could observe in a lifetime.

The Apollo landing sites cannot be seen with a telescope. If the smallest crater visible is half a mile across, what chance is there to see pieces of hardware the size of a family station wagon?

Chapter Five

✦

OBSERVING SOLAR AND LUNAR ECLIPSES

As interesting as the sun and moon are, they are incomparably more fascinating when they align and one darkens. A rare sun-earth-moon alignment creates one of the most magnificent spectacles in nature.

Eclipses come in two "flavors," solar and lunar. A solar eclipse happens when the moon blocks and eclipses the light of the sun, darkening it. A lunar eclipse happens when the moon moves into the shadow of the earth and therefore darkens. Several eclipses happen each year, but solar eclipses seem much rarer because they can be seen only from a particular part of the earth—the part within the moon's shadow—while an eclipse of the moon can be seen simultaneously by everyone on the half of the earth facing the moon. Both kinds can be either partial or total, and in all cases, a total eclipse is more interesting than is a partial eclipse.

Eclipse of the Sun

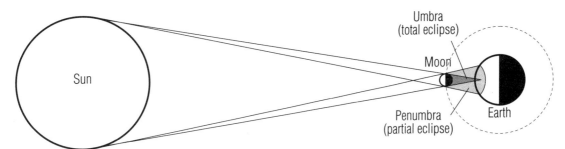

A solar eclipse happens when the moon moves in front of and blocks the sun.

LUNAR ECLIPSES

At least twice and sometimes three times each year, the full moon moves into the shadow of the earth and grows dark for up to a few hours. While everyone on the side of the earth facing the moon sees the eclipse simultaneously, their location determines whether they are seeing it during the evening, late at night, or early in the morning. (You cannot see a daytime lunar eclipse because only the full moon is eclipsed, and the full moon lies opposite the sun and is always below the horizon when the sun is above.)

First, let's understand what happens when the moon moves into the shadow of the earth. A shadow is surprisingly complex.

There are two parts to every shadow: the dark central *umbra* and the lighter surrounding *penumbra*. Look at this first from a position on the moon. If you are standing on the moon within the earth's umbra, the sun is completely blocked by the earth and the eclipse is total at your location. But if you are standing within the penumbra, the sun is only partially blocked and the eclipse is partial at your location. As seen from the earth, the part of the moon in the penumbra is slightly darkened, because some sunlight is still striking it, while the part in the umbra is very dark. Each eclipse is different, and all are not equally interesting.

The darkness of an eclipse depends on whether the moon moves into the penumbra alone or into the umbra partially or fully—called, respectively, *penumbral*, *partial*, and *total*. In a *penumbral* eclipse, the moon moves within the penumbra of the earth's shadow but does not enter the umbra; the moon darkens very little, making penumbral eclipses hard to see. During a *partial* eclipse, only part of the moon moves within the umbra, and that part darkens dramatically. Although the moon does not disappear, partial eclipses are definitely worth watching. A *total* eclipse happens when the moon moves fully within the umbra; the entire moon goes dark and sometimes even disappears. Grand sky spectacles, total lunar eclipses are not to be missed.

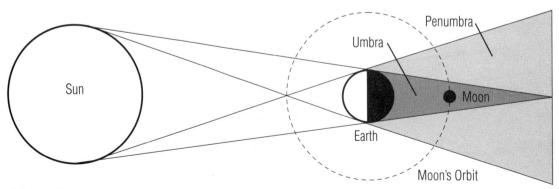

A lunar eclipse is an eclipse of the moon; it occurs when the moon moves through the shadow of the earth and darkens.

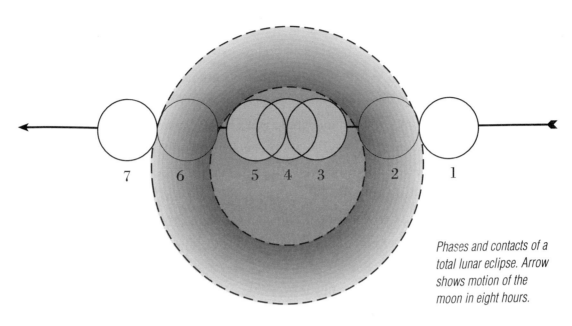

Phases and contacts of a total lunar eclipse. Arrow shows motion of the moon in eight hours.

An eclipse happens as a sequence of stages. (The time of each stage is usually noted in newspapers and science magazines, although penumbral eclipses often are not announced.) In a penumbral eclipse, the moon moves into the penumbra and then moves out again, and generally no one even notices. In a partial eclipse, briefly, (1) moon moves into penumbra; (2) moon moves into umbra; (3) maximum eclipse; (4) moon leaves umbra; (5) moon leaves penumbra. A total eclipse adds two more stages for a total of seven: (1) moon moves into penumbra; (2) moon begins to move into umbra; (3) moon is completely within umbra (totality begins); (4) maximum eclipse; (5) moon begins to leave umbra; (6) moon completely leaves umbra (totality ends); (7) moon leaves penumbra. An eclipse is "total" during the time the moon is completely within the umbra (stages 3 to 5), and that is the best time to watch.

The most interesting eclipses, not surprisingly, are total. Only then does the moon darken enough to take on a ghostly appearance or even to disappear, and only then does it exhibit strange, eerie colors.

During a lunar eclipse, the moon often becomes orange or deep red. The moon is lit only by sunlight, which is pure white, so where do these garish colors come from? They are produced by sunlight refracted around the edge of the earth and onto the moon. When white sunlight enters the earth's atmosphere, most is refracted and scattered away. Blue light scatters best, which is why the sky is blue. Red light passes through our atmosphere relatively unaffected (it is refracted least), which is why sunrises and sunsets appear red. Unrefracted, reddened sunlight passes through the atmosphere at the edge of the earth—where the earth's sunrises and sunsets happen—and continues on to the moon to give it its reddish color; all the light that reaches the moon is tinted by the earth's sunrises and sunsets.

During some total lunar eclipses, the moon takes on a pale orange color but remains relatively bright. At other times, the moon becomes so deep a shade of red that it disappears and cannot be seen, even in binoculars. Sunsets display the same variation—some are dull and some are breathtaking. The relative color and brightness of a lunar eclipse depends on similar atmospheric conditions. If conditions are clear and dry in that part of the atmosphere at the earth's edge where sunlight is refracted, the moon reddens little and the eclipse appears bright. If, however, there is much dust in that same part of the atmosphere, the eclipse is redder and darker. Major volcanic eruptions, such as of the Philippine's Mt. Pinatubo in 1991, throw high into the atmosphere massive amounts of dust, which linger for years and cause eclipses that follow to be incredibly dark. Eclipses are as variable as the weather, making their appearance not fully predictable. This adds interest, because while we can forecast the appearance of an eclipse to some degree, there is no way to be sure what you'll see except to watch.

In contrast to a solar eclipse, no filters or special precautions are needed to observe a lunar eclipse. After all, the eclipsed moon is just a huge gray rock in the shade! Watch with binoculars or a telescope to bring out the colors.

As the drama of a lunar eclipse slowly unfolds, there are several things to watch for. Let's "walk through" a total eclipse. If the moon is above the horizon before the eclipse begins, notice its brightness. The moon is several times brighter when completely full than even one day before or after, when it *looks* full, so take a moment to notice how very bright the completely full moon is. At the time the moon enters the penumbra of the earth's shadow (which you can pinpoint thanks to announcements in the newspaper or from a local planetarium or science museum), see if you can tell that the moon has begun to darken. The effect is very subtle, and the actual edge of the penumbra cannot be detected. Is one side of the moon darker than another, and by how much? By the time the moon begins to enter the umbra, however, it is clear which side of the moon is deepest in shadow. Because the earth's umbra has a relatively sharp edge, you will notice when the moon crosses its boundary. Now it looks as if the moon has a bite taken out of it! Is there color to the umbra? (Probably not yet, because of the bright sunlight falling on the rest of the moon.) When do you first notice hints of color, and is the color orange or red? As the moon moves progressively deeper into the umbra, the "bite" grows and the curvature of the umbra's edge becomes apparent. Does the darkening moon make it easier to see faint stars?

TOTAL LUNAR ECLIPSES
VISIBLE FROM NORTH AMERICA

2000 Jan. 21	2014 Apr. 15
2001 Jan. 9	2014 Oct. 8
2003 May 16	2015 Apr. 4
2003 Nov. 9	2015 Sep. 28
2004 Oct. 28	2018 Jan. 31
2007 Mar. 3	2019 Jan. 21
2007 Aug. 28	2021 May 26
2008 Feb. 21	2022 May 16
2010 Dec. 21	2022 Nov. 8
2011 Dec. 10	2025 Mar. 14

This table lists total lunar eclipses through the year 2025, visible from at least part of North America. Some occur in the evening, others in the morning. Additionally, a few partial eclipses (not listed here) are visible during these years.

Monitor the sky around the moon to watch stars appear as the moon's light wanes and the sky darkens. You can read a book by the light of the full moon; when is the sky too dark to read by moonlight? By watching the moon move deeper into the umbra, can you predict how dark it will be during totality, and what its color will be then? When only a sliver of moon is left outside the umbra, the moon takes on a very odd shape, and whatever color it will have should now be apparent. When does the moon stop casting a shadow? You can time the moment of the onset of totality to within a minute or two just by watching. How dark is the moon during totality? What is its color, and is the color uniform across the moon's face? Which (if any) major features on the moon can you still recognize? How dark has the sky become, and can you see faint stars and even the Milky Way? If the moon does not move directly through the center of the umbra, one side will be brighter than the other. Can you anticipate, by subtle changes in the shading, when totality will end? How do the colors fade as brightness returns? When can you again begin to discern the moon's major surface features? When do faint stars fade to invisibility as the sky brightens? The last stages of the eclipse, mirroring its early stages, are an anticlimax, but by now you may be thinking anyway about going to bed!

When an eclipse takes place while the moon is rising or setting, there is the bonus of a moonrise (or moonset) and additional reddening resulting from light reflected off the eclipsed moon passing through our atmosphere a second time. Excellent photo opportunities also present themselves when the eclipsed moon appears near features on the horizon.

Make an attempt to watch the entire eclipse, even if at intervals, to appreciate the many changes that occur. An eclipse is a process that unfolds, not a momentary event.

SOLAR ECLIPSES

No celestial spectacle (including a world-class sunset) is as sensational as a total solar eclipse. In the past, battles have halted and brave men trembled when the sun went dark during the day. Even today in many areas of the world there is general panic and great alarm. Animals have been known to alter their behavior during an eclipse. A number of people travel great distances at great expense to see one, and it fills that year's vacation schedule. Some people are affected at a deep emotional level. No one carries on business as usual.

Paradoxically, there are more solar than lunar eclipses in an average year—four or five solar versus two or three lunar—but solar eclipses are seen by far fewer people. This is due to the relative sizes of the shadows of the earth and moon. The earth is so large that the umbra of its shadow can easily engulf the moon, and when it does, everyone on the side of the earth facing the moon can together watch the eclipse. The much smaller umbra of the moon barely reaches the earth, and when it does, it has a width of no more than 167 miles, and often much less. The moon's shadow traces out a long thin path, called the "path of totality," which moves across the earth's surface, and only the relatively few people within this path see the eclipse as total. Far more see the eclipse as a less interesting partial. Because the shadow is moving quickly, totality lasts for no more than a few minutes. Nevertheless, people will pay $1,000 per minute to stand in the moon's shadow.

It is one of nature's great coincidences that the moon is 400 times smaller than the

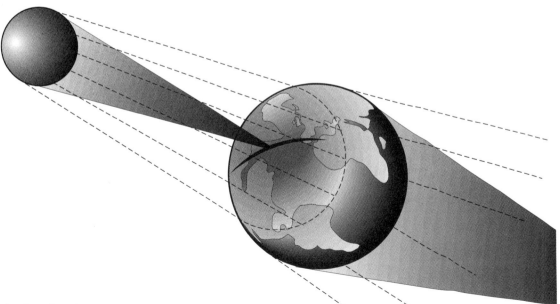

A solar eclipse is seen as partial from much of the earth, but only people within a narrow path see it as total.

Partial, Annular, and Total Solar Eclipses

sun but 400 times closer to the earth, so the sun and moon have the same *apparent size* in the sky (each is ½ degree in diameter). This coincidence allows the moon to cover the sun, but just barely. Were the moon a little smaller or a little more distant, it would fail to cover the sun and there would be no total solar eclipses. Were it much closer or much larger, it would block not only the disk of the sun but also its wispy corona, which gives a total eclipse so much of its beauty.

Just as there are different types of lunar eclipses and several stages in each, there are different types of solar eclipses. Let's begin by considering each kind.

Just as the earth's shadow has an outer penumbra and an inner umbra, so does the moon's shadow. When you stand on the earth in the moon's umbra, the moon completely blocks the sun and you are in darkness; the eclipse it total. When you stand in the penumbra, the moon blocks only part of the sun so that a crescent of the sun's disk remains to shine around the edge of the moon; the eclipse is partial. All total eclipses are partial in their initial and final stages.

Partial and total solar eclipses have their lunar counterparts, but there is a third type of solar eclipse that is unique. The moon's average distance from the earth may enable it to completely—though barely—cover the sun, but its orbit is not truly round; maximum and minimum distances are 252,700 and 221,500 miles, respectively. If an eclipse happens while the moon is at the more distant points in its orbit, the moon does not appear large enough to completely cover the sun. Instead, it is superimposed on the face of the sun, blocking most of the sun's disk but leaving a ring of sunlight to shine around the moon's edge. Such a "ring" eclipse is called *annular*, after the Latin word for "ring." It is rather unusual to see the sun as a thin ring in the sky, and although the sky does not grow as dark as in a total eclipse nor are there all the auxiliary phenomena, annular eclipses are interesting in their own right.

✦ TOTAL ECLIPSES ✦

Total eclipses are the rage in astronomy today, but none will occur in the distant future. The moon is slowly receding from the earth at the rate of 1½ inches per year—roughly the rate at which your fingernails grow. Its angular size is diminishing proportionately. Today, the moon barely covers the sun. To our distant descendants, total solar eclipses will be a thing of the past. They will enjoy annular eclipses only. The last total solar eclipse will happen in the year 600,000,000 A.D.

Most eclipses you will see are partial. You must be within the narrow path of totality to see a total eclipse, but for about 2,000 miles on either side, everyone sees what looks like a bite being taken out of the sun. The closer you are to the center-line, the bigger the bite appears. People on several continents see the eclipse as partial.

When the sun is partially blocked by the moon, the part that remains shines as bright as always. Even when 90 percent of the sun is eclipsed, the remaining 10 percent is too intense for human eyes. You must take special effort to view the partially eclipsed sun safely. The filters and projection techniques described under "Observing the Sun" on page 23 will show the sun's face in great detail, complete with sunspots if any are present. But to see merely the shape of the partially eclipsed sun requires only very basic equipment.

The old standby is a pinhole viewing box. This is especially popular with schools, perhaps because it involves simple hands-on construction. Begin with a shoe box or similar small box not of too coarse a cardboard, and discard the lid. In one end of the box, cut away a small section roughly a square inch in size, and tape a piece of tinfoil over the resulting hole. Punch a pinhole in this foil. A large pinhole gives a brighter but fuzzier image than does a smaller pinhole, which casts a fainter but sharper shadow; live a little, and punch several of different sizes. Tape a piece of white paper (a 3 × 5 file card works well) on the inside of the opposite end of the box. Hold the box, now an "eclipse viewer," so sunlight falls through the pinhole and onto the card, where the sun's image will appear. Orient your view so the box shades the card. (This is an ideal project for third-graders.)

Even simpler and more effective is to use a mirror to reflect the sun's image onto the north-facing wall of a building. Smaller mirrors give fainter images and must be closer to the wall (several tens of feet); large mirrors a foot square can be 100 feet or more away and still reflect a brilliant image. Attach the mirror to something solid, fasten a large sheet of smooth white cardboard on the wall, and *voilà*! You have a first-class image that can be viewed by a crowd and even photographed with standard cameras.

These special techniques are needed only when the sun is partially eclipsed (that includes annular eclipses). For the few moments when the sun is totally eclipsed, its surface is completely blocked by the moon and the part that remains visible—its outer corona—is not too bright to look at directly. (That is why we see the corona only during an eclipse; normally, it is overwhelmed by bright sunlight.) At totality then, set aside filters, projection boxes, and mirrors, and watch the sun in all its glory. The sun appears surprisingly small, so use binoculars or a low-power telescope. Tripod-mounted binoculars are ideal for a total eclipse because they encompass the entire corona, which spans several degrees; the corona is too large to fit within the field of view of a telescope. Be sure to turn your binoculars or telescope away when totality ends, an event that fortunately does not happen too abruptly for you to have adequate warning.

A partial eclipse is not a complicated affair. Nevertheless, prepare and test your filters or projection box in advance, especially if you will be viewing the eclipse with others. The moment the eclipse begins, you will notice a notch missing from the sun's edge. That notch grows slowly until maximum eclipse, and then it diminishes. If using a telescope, you might notice sunspots being eclipsed and then reappearing adding a bit of novelty to an otherwise drawn-out event. High magnification will reveal the true measure of the moon's roughness. Prepare to see the profile of craters and mountains starkly silhouetted against the sun.

If more than half the sun is covered, it takes on a curious crescent shape—a shape we don't usually associate with that body. Pinholes, in fact, cast crescent-shaped shadows. Look for bright little shimmering crescents under trees where overlapping leaves create natural pinholes.

If the eclipse is nearly total (as it is in all annular eclipses), how much does the sky darken? Does it merely become a deeper shade of blue? Look at the shadows around you, which appear somehow different.

If the eclipse takes place at sunrise or sunset, all its added effects are thrown in—at no extra cost. At sunrise or sunset, a partial or annular eclipse can be quite spectacular, second only to a total eclipse.

A total eclipse includes all the features of a partial eclipse plus the glorious brief moments of totality. As totality approaches, it begins to feel like an impending storm. The sky grows darker, the temperature begins to drop, and a slight breeze may start to stir and

The total solar eclipse of 1991. Photograph by Bruce M. Gottlieb.

possibly even build to a pronounced wind. People seldom observe a total eclipse alone, and the general excitement and anticipation in the air can reach dizzying levels.

About ten minutes before totality, eerie bands of light may ripple over the landscape. They pass mysteriously over people, trees, and houses, as though borne by the wind itself. These "shadow bands" are an atmospheric phenomena that have never been satisfactorily explained.

The moon's shadow approaches from the west, darkening the sky from that direction. This darkening accelerates during the last minutes before totality, and very soon the ultra-thin crescent of sunlight shatters into an array of brilliant beads. These are produced by sunlight passing through valleys and other depressions along the moon's edge. Finally, one bead may remain, creating a dazzling "diamond ring" effect. The diamond shrinks to nothingness before you have time to catch your breath. Totality has arrived, and the corona with its quiet majesty shines down upon us.

The sky, though dark, is not a midnight sky with its myriad stars; it's a deep twilight, with only the planets and brighter stars visible. If you have plotted in advance the positions of planets and bright stars relative to the sun, you can observe them briefly. You might even glimpse a comet! The horizon remains bright in the distance, a brightness that swiftly shifts from east to west as the center of the shadow passes eastward.

The light of the sun's corona is usually described as white with a bluish tinge, and it can be rich in delicate structure. If you look toward the edge of the moon with binoculars, you may catch sight of reddish prominences hovering above the sun.

TOTAL SOLAR ECLIPSES

Date	Location
1999 Aug. 11	Europe, Iran, India
2001 Jun. 21	South Africa
2002 Dec. 4	South Africa, southern Indian Ocean
2006 Mar. 29	Africa, Mediterranean, Turkey, Ukraine, Siberia
2009 Jul. 22	China, western Pacific Ocean
2012 Nov. 13	Northern Australia, South Pacific
2016 Mar. 9	Indonesia, western Pacific
2017 Aug. 21	United States, from Oregon to South Carolina
2019 Jul. 2	Chile, Argentina
2020 Dec. 14	Chile, Argentina
2024 Apr. 8	Mexico, the United States from Texas to New England, Newfoundland

This table lists major total solar eclipses through the year 2025. It omits partial eclipses and total eclipses visible only from inaccessible parts of the earth. Eclipses over warmer oceans are visited by specially chartered cruise ships on popular "eclipse expeditions."

All too quickly, a brilliant jewel of light appears at the outer edge of the moon's limb, announcing the end of totality. The phenomena previously seen now repeat themselves in reverse order, until once again the sun is brightly shining, and the eclipse just a memory.

Don't forget to take photographs. Even if you are not equipped with the specialized equipment needed to capture the delicate shadings of the corona, all those shots of excited people make a great souvenir! If you have a video camera, let it run continuously for the sound, if nothing else.

Everyone who experiences a total eclipse of the sun comes away feeling a great sense of privilege at having been present at such a dramatic and awe-inspiring event. One gets the feeling of having come face to face with the forces of the cosmos.

Several sites on the World Wide Web provide very detailed information on eclipses, both solar and lunar, major and minor, far into the future. Begin with the Eclipse Home Page at http://planets.gsfc.nasa.gov/eclipse/eclipse.html or the U.S. Naval Observatory's Upcoming Eclipses site at http://riemann.usno.navy.mil/AA/data/docs/UpcomingEclipses.html.

Chapter Six

✦

OBSERVING THE PLANETS

Without a telescope, the planets appear to be slowly moving dots of light. They are in constant motion as they wander from constellation to constellation. Sometimes they pass one another in a conjunction, group together in a massing, or are eclipsed by the moon. All these phenomena are fun to watch. Fortunately, it takes nothing beyond an awareness of what is happening and a cloud-free night to enjoy the nightly parade of the planets. (See, by the same author and publisher, *Stargazing for Beginners* and, for young readers, *The Ultimate Guide to the Sky* for an understanding of how the sky changes nightly and how the planets move among the stars.)

This book, however, assumes you are observing the planets with a telescope; it also assumes you already know which planet is which. For help in identifying which planets are visible on a given night, check the sky calendars of monthly astronomy magazines such as *Astronomy* and *Sky & Telescope*.

Most of what you will look at in the sky does not withstand much magnification. The best views of the Milky Way, comets, and bright star clusters are available with binoculars or a low-power wide-angle telescope. Planets, however, appear so tiny (because of their distances) that to view them in any detail requires a telescope with quality optics and a stable mounting capable of high magnification. The minimum is a 3-inch refractor or 5-inch reflector, although much depends on quality. Inexpensive toy store telescopes show little beyond the moons of Jupiter and the outline of the rings of Saturn.

A night with steady air is also essential, although a dark sky is not; you can observe the planets as readily from the city as from the country. Nor does bright moonlight interfere. Do avoid looking at the planets when they are near the horizon, where atmospheric turbulence is ruinous. On many nights, the air may be so unsteady that there is nothing you can do but abandon the planets for viewing other things. Nights when the air is calm and images are therefore sharp are nights to treasure.

Even with a good telescope, you must practice seeing. People who glance quickly at Jupiter through a telescope will miss the subtle shading and color gradations that give the planet its wealth of detail. Features on Mars, Jupiter, and Saturn are also subtle, and it takes time to tease them out. You must look and think critically and to focus your attention.

THE PLANETS' MOTIONS AND THE ZODIAC

The planet Earth moves around the sun in one Earth year (365¼ days). Each planet orbits the sun in its period of time, which ranges from 88 Earth days for Mercury to 248 Earth years for Pluto. We can watch the planets move around the sky at various speeds, traveling from constellation to constellation.

Because the solar system is nearly flat and the planets' orbits all lie in nearly the same plane, we see their orbits essentially edge-on. Were we to look down on the solar system from above, we would see the planets move around the sun on nearly circular orbits. From our vantage point *within* the solar system and in the plane of the orbits, however, the planets appear to move back and forth along the line that marks the plane of the solar system. That line, called the *ecliptic*, is the orbit of the earth projected into space. It is identical to the apparent path of the sun through the sky. The sun remains on it, and the moon and planets stay near it. The important point is that, because the solar system is flat, the planets and the moon stay close to the path of the sun.

The constellations the sun passes through are known as the constellations of the *zodiac*. Although they are well-known, many of them are not conspicuous, and contain no bright stars. For example, Aquarius has no bright stars; it is famous because of *where* it is, rather than *what* it is (which is a bunch of faint stars, lacking any easily recognizable shape).

The zodiac was invented in Babylon about 2,600 years ago. It was divided into the 12 traditional constellations, although the sun actually passes through 13 using modern constellation boundaries. There are therefore 13 constellations of the astronomical zodiac: Capricornus, Aquarius, Pisces, Aries, Taurus, Gemini, Cancer, Leo, Virgo, Libra, Scorpius, Ophiuchus, and Sagittarius. The amount of time the sun spends in each depends on the constellation's width, which differs for each constellation.

The planets orbit the sun in the same direction as the earth does (counterclockwise as seen from above the solar system's north pole). They would appear to move from west to east in the sky, as the moon does, were our view not complicated by our earth's own motion. To understand the motion of the planets in the sky, it is best to divide them into two groups: those orbiting inside the earth's orbit (Mercury and Venus) and those orbiting outside our orbit (all the rest). Planets in the first group are called "inferior," and those in the other, "superior."

Inferior planets remain in the vicinity of the sun and appear either in front of the sun, behind it, or a short distance to the east or west. They cannot be seen when they are in front of or behind the sun, of course; when they are to one side, they appear in either the morning or evening sky. Mercury remains so close to the sun (no more than 28 degrees) it is visible only in twilight, and even then it never appears far from the horizon. The challenge in observing Mercury is simply to find it. Venus, poetically referred to as "the morning star" as well as the "evening star," can stray up to 47 degrees from the sun and be seen against a dark sky, but it too is usually visible in twilight.

Both Mercury and Venus proceed through cycles that begin when they are between the earth and sun; at that time, they are in front of the sun and invisible. They then move to the right (west) of the sun, rise before the sun, and appear in the morning sky. Their visibility improves as their angular distance from the sun increases until they reach their maximum angular separation from the sun (called "maximum elongation" in almanacs). Then, receding from the earth, they swing around to the far side of the sun, disappearing from view before aligning behind the sun (when they cannot be seen again; when directly behind the sun they are at "superior conjunction"). They then move eastward and to the left of the sun, appearing in the evening sky. Because they are on the far side of the sun when they begin their evening appearance, their relative motion in the sky is slow and they reappear gradually. Their visibility in the evening sky improves daily until they eventually reach their maximum eastward angular separation from the sun. The cycle is completed when they move back in front of the sun. Because they are then close to the earth and their apparent motion is at its greatest, they disappear from the evening sky relatively rapidly.

The outer "superior" planets cannot move between the earth and sun, but they can position themselves on the sun's far side. A planet on the far side of the sun is said to be at "superior conjunction," and it cannot be seen then. It is the *earth* that moves between the sun and a superior planet, and when it does, that planet lies opposite the sun and is at "opposition." A planet at opposition is at its closest to the earth and at its brightest and largest. Being opposite the sun, it rises at sunset and is visible all night long.

Superior planets would move only eastward around the sun and against the background of stars were it not for the fact that the earth moves faster on its inside orbit. Our speedier motion causes us to "pass" each outer planet, and for a few months, the earth's more rapid motion makes it appear as if the planet we are passing is moving backward against the stars. This westward or "retrograde" motion is an illusion; the outer planets do not actually back up in their orbits, but they appear to do so as seen from the earth. You see the same effect when you pass a slower-moving car on the freeway—it *appears* to move backward as seen against distant trees and hills, but you are simply moving forward at a greater speed. Each planet is in retrograde motion as we pass it, and once we have moved on, the planet appears to resume its normal eastward motion. Hence each outer planet apparently makes a backward loop in the sky each year as we overtake it and move on ahead.

Most of the planets look like bright stars and are therefore easy to recognize. Mercury, however, is seen only near the horizon during morning or evening twilight, and takes extra knowledge to find. Uranus, Neptune, and Pluto are too faint to see without a telescope and detailed charts.

MERCURY

The challenge with Mercury is to see it at all. Mercury spends most of its time in front of or behind the sun or else too near to it to be seen. Only when it is at its greatest angular separation from the sun does it appear in the morning or evening sky, near the horizon. When in the morning sky, Mercury rises shortly before the sun and is quickly lost in the coming dawn; when in the evening sky, it is glimpsed during twilight but then sets before the sky becomes fully dark. An unobstructed horizon is essential.

Mercury, like our moon, goes through a cycle of phases. When Mercury is between the earth and sun, it is in its new phase—which we cannot see. When behind the sun, it is full—which we cannot see either. We see Mercury only when it is to the left or right of the sun and at or near its quarter phase. Then it looks like a surprisingly tiny half-moon. Because Mercury is always seen near the horizon, we view it through the thickest and most turbulent layers of our atmosphere; this turbulence usually prevents us from seeing the planet clearly enough to discern its phase.

Ironically, Mercury is one of only two planets whose surface is visible (the other is Mars). Yet although it has no atmosphere of its own to generate obscuring clouds, it is too small and distant for its surface markings to be observable from the earth regardless of the size of the telescope used. Most of our information about Mercury's surface comes from a spacecraft that flew by it decades ago.

About a dozen times each century, Mercury passes directly in front of the sun and "transits" the sun's disk, looking like a very small and slowly moving sunspot. The next transits of Mercury are in November 1999, May 2003, November 2006, May 2016, November 2019, and November 2032. Check an astronomy magazine then for details. You need the same equipment to see a transit of Mercury as you do to see sunspots (see "Observing the Sun," p. 23).

VENUS

Venus is loveliest with the naked eye. It appears during daybreak or twilight when the sky is at its most colorful, and the sight of this dazzlingly brilliant white point of light among the colors of sunset is one of the more sublime sights in nature.

Venus appears and then disappears in a cycle that lasts most of a year. When it makes its appearance in the evening sky, it slowly gains altitude day by day until it can be seen well after sunset. It then loses altitude relatively rapidly, dropping from sight in a few weeks as it moves between the earth and sun. It reappears a few weeks later in the morning sky, where it quickly gains height. Then it loses altitude day by day as it travels away from the earth and around to the far side of the sun. Five hundred and eighty-four days after first appearing in the evening sky, it is back again to begin another cycle.

Although attractive to the naked eye, there is little to see on Venus through a telescope. Nevertheless, as Galileo discovered four centuries ago, even the smallest telescopes will show its phases. Because it changes phase slowly, you can easily observe its rise or decline from one week to the next.

Venus changes its apparent size more than any other planet, and that too can be monitored. Notice how much smaller it appears when on the far side of the sun than when near to the earth and a comparatively huge crescent.

Venus has the color of pure reflected sunlight, which is white (not the yellow we sometimes think it is). Any color that appears in it is caused by dust in our own atmosphere. A dense layer of clouds permanently shrouds the planet, preventing us from seeing its many volcanic surface features. This smooth cloud layer reflects sunlight very efficiently, which is one reason Venus appears so bright in our sky (the other is that it comes so close to our own planet).

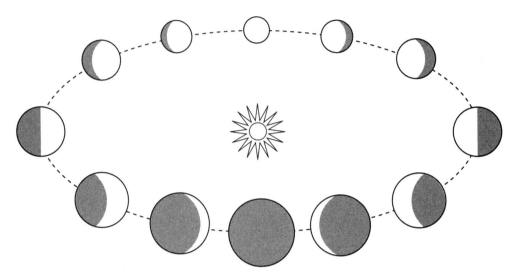

Mercury and Venus change both their apparent size and phase as they orbit the sun.

Try to locate Venus during the daytime. If the sky is free of moisture and dust (you can tell by the sky's color—a deep blue sky is clear, an off-white one is not), you can see Venus with your eyes alone if you know where to look. Notice how far Venus is to the east of the setting sun (or to the west of the rising sun); the following day, look that same distance either east or west of the sun. Binoculars make the task easy, and Venus shows up surprisingly well in the daytime through a low-power telescope. It is wise to position yourself in the shadow of a house or building blocking the sun so that you do not inadvertently glance at the sun while hunting for Venus.

On widely separated occasions, Venus transits the sun. The only two transits during the 21st century are on June 8, 2004 (visible from Europe but not the United States) and June 6, 2012 (the beginning will be visible from the United States). These rare events will be detailed in popular astronomy magazines as the time approaches. For people with properly filtered telescopes, Venus will look like a black dot slowly moving across the sun's face.

MARS

More than any other planet, Mars captures our imaginations. To observe its surface features through a telescope, however, is a true challenge. It is comparatively small and far away (twice the diameter of our moon but at least a hundred times more distant), and many people are disappointed the first time they see it through a telescope.

Most of the time, Mars is too distant and too small for meaningful telescopic observation. But once every 26 months on the average, when Mars is at "opposition" (opposite the sun) and the earth slowly passes it, the two planets are relatively close. Mars consequently

MARS OPPOSITIONS

1999 April	2014 April
2001 June	2016 May
2003 August	2018 July
2005 November	2020 October
2007 December	2022 December
2010 January	2025 January
2012 March	2027 February

appears far larger than normal, although "large" is of course a relative term. Amateurs seize the opportunity then to turn their telescopes toward it for a few months and essentially ignore it the rest of the time.

When Mars is closest to the earth and opposite the sun, we see it in its full phase. When farthest from the earth and closest to the sun (in angular measure), it is in its gibbous phase. At the beginning and end of each opposition period, when Mars is southeast in the morning sky or southwest in the evening sky, about all you can see through a good telescope is its pronounced noncircular shape.

This table lists dates when Mars is closest to the earth through 2028. Mars is at its best for viewing two months before and two months after these dates.

Without a telescope, Mars is an orange "star" that wanders among the constellations of the zodiac. When at its nearest to the earth, it is brighter than any star, second in brilliance only to Jupiter and Venus (and occasionally outshining Jupiter). Unlike Jupiter and Saturn, which orbit the sun so slowly they remain in the same constellation for a year or more, Mars moves relatively swiftly, sometimes crossing a constellation in one month. It often passes near a bright star or even in front of a star cluster, and its comparatively rapid movement makes it more fun to track by eye than any other planet.

Mars is the only planet whose surface features we see through a telescope. Most of its surface is a rocky desert broken here and there by volcanoes and impact craters. Broad dark areas, which superficially resemble the seas on the moon, identify places where the covering of dust is thin, allowing darker bedrock to show through; light areas reveal where dust is either thicker or fresher. The most prominent dark features usually are Syrtis Major and Mare Acidalium. Individual craters and volcanoes are too small to see from the earth, but the planet's light and dark markings have been charted for more than a century. Do not be surprised, however, if Mars as you see it differs from how it appears on published maps, since the light and dark markings change shape and intensity somewhat from year to year.

The most conspicuous Martian surface features are its two polar caps, one at the north pole and one at the south. One or the other (depending on how the planet is tilted) shines

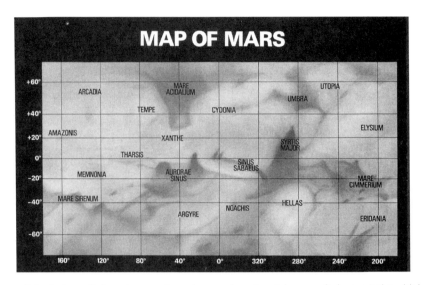

This map shows all the features that can be seen through a good amateur telescope. It does not show high latitudes and the polar caps. Drawn by the author with an 8-inch Newtonian reflector.

brightly as a tiny white spot at the planet's north or south edge. Mars, like the earth, is tilted and has seasons (although they're twice as long, since its year is twice as long), and the planet's polar caps grow and shrink seasonally. If you follow the planet for several months, you can watch one cap grow as the other one shrinks. Usually only one cap is conspicuous. The polar caps form each winter under a hood of white frost that can be bright enough to be confused with the ice cap itself.

Often as bright as the polar caps are the Hellas and Argyre Basins—two huge circular impact craters that appear very bright when covered with frost. Hellas is 1,000 miles across and Argyre about a third that dimension.

A red or orange filter can improve viewing by heightening contrast, making the dark areas appear darker. A blue filter brings out the clouds.

The side of Mars that faces the earth changes as Mars rotates. A day on Mars is only slightly longer than a day on Earth—24 hours 37.5 minutes—and during the course of a night, you can watch Mars rotate more than a third of the way. Features that rotate into view early in the evening are centered on the planet around midnight and rotate out of view by dawn. The following night, those same features rotate into view 37.5 minutes later. During the course of a few weeks, each face of Mars is visible in succession, and after 36 Earth days, Mars returns to the same orientation at the same time of night.

Mars maps and tables will let you identify the side of Mars facing the earth at any given moment. The meridian (longitude) on Mars, centered on the planet as viewed from the earth, is called the "central meridian." You can look up the longitude of the central meridian in popular astronomy magazines when Mars is close to the earth and know which side of the planet you are observing.

Dust storms, both local and global, begin when the planet warms sufficiently. While local dust storms obscure only small areas of the planet, a global storm can leave the entire planet featureless for months at a time. Major dust storms are more common during the Martian summer, when warm air kicks wind-borne dust high into the atmosphere, where it settles only very slowly. Many start in the Hellas Basin.

In the late 1800s, astronomers discovered that a number of surface markings, especially around the poles, change intensity with the seasons. In the spring and summer, as a polar ice cap evaporates, nearby features become progressively darker in a "wave of darkening" that spreads to lower latitudes. For the first half of the 20th century, these seasonal changes were considered strong evidence for life on Mars; the darkening was believed to represent plant cover, which then disappeared with the change of season and the death of the plant life. Now we know, however, that such changes in Mars's appearance result when the fierce winds that blow each spring distribute light-colored dust far and wide, so that what was interpreted as a darkening of some areas is actually a brightening of others as they are deposited with fresh dust. Such changes will not be noticed by an observer who only glances at Mars from time to time, but a mindful observer with a good telescope who returns to the planet regularly can follow such changes through the Martian seasons.

Mars's two tiny moons, meanwhile, are visible only with the largest amateur telescopes.

When observing Mars, the importance of steady air becomes evident. To see Mars as more than a small orange dot, you must use high magnification, and high magnification can only be used effectively when the earth's air is steady. When our atmosphere is turbulent, as it often is on a cold night, it blurs images as seen through a telescope. Therefore, pick an observing location where you are not looking across objects that absorbed the sun's heat during the day to then radiate it at night (like a house roof or any sort of pavement); look instead across a lawn or garden. On many clear nights you will have to abandon Mars because the air is not steady, and even on the best nights, moments of good viewing come and go quickly. Be prepared to watch Mars intently for ten minutes or more, capturing the rare second here and there of greatest clarity. Features will swim into focus and then blur again just as suddenly, and you will see the planet's delicate markings only for a moment at a time. Patience is the key—along with quality optics.

JUPITER

Jupiter has more surface area and, not surprisingly then, shows more surface features than all the other planets combined. Its major bands and belts can be seen in even the smallest telescopes. Plus it offers a bonus of four bright moons that continuously change their position.

The giant planets from Jupiter on out are made largely of gas or ice, and—with the exception of Pluto—they have no solid surface. We see only the top of enormously thick atmospheres. Jupiter's atmosphere is especially colorful, and the planet's rapid rotation blurs cloud features into long, narrow bands paralleling its equator, which appear to swathe it. Details within the bands change from month to month and from year to year, and the bands themselves alternately grow and diminish in width and intensity. The foremost feature of Jupiter, however, is its series of alternating dark cloud bands and light cloud belts. The dark bands are regions where we look deep into the atmosphere and see to warmer depths, while the lighter belts represent higher and colder clouds.

While Jupiter's atmosphere (and indeed the whole planet) is mostly hydrogen plus a smaller amount of helium, the clouds themselves are made of molecules of heavier gases such as ammonia and methane. Their colors result from minor and more complex chemicals whose compositions are not yet well understood. Jupiter's bands and zones are designated in a code that represents latitude (the STrZ, for example, is the South Tropical Zone). The following diagram shows the planet's basic appearance, but be aware that the contents of the features shown are endlessly variable.

Jupiter's most famous feature is undoubtedly the Great Red Spot, an elliptical cloud three times the size of the earth, which has been identified since at least the early 1800s and probably much earlier. It is a semipermanent eddy or vortex colored by complex organic molecules that lies on the south edge of Jupiter's South Equatorial Belt, cutting somewhat into that feature. The appearance of the Great Red Spot changes significantly from year to year. At times it is deep red and visible in even a 2-inch refracting telescope; at other times it fades into the background and virtually disappears, leaving behind the Red Spot Hollow. Smaller (not "great") red spots also come and go, as do many small white spots. Ovals may also exist in great number. Festoons extending from the dark bands into the lighter belts can be surprisingly delicate, and thin white clouds may cross dark bands.

As in the case of Mars, the more you look, the more you see. Jupiter's major bands and zones are visible through almost any telescope, but its more delicate cloud features take

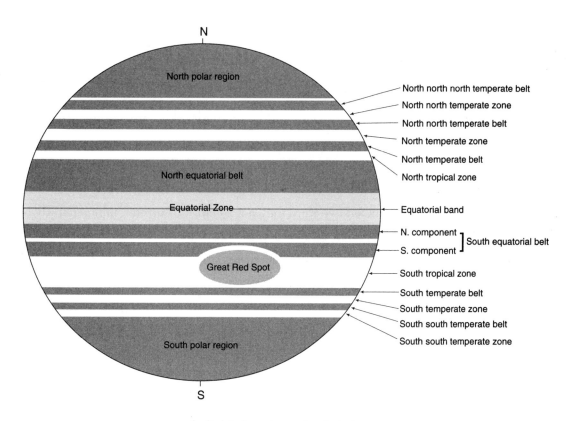

Jupiter's belts and zones in a typical year.

more effort to see. Minor features are so numerous that on a night with steady air it seems impossible to absorb or to sketch all that you see through a good telescope. Notice the colors as well as the shapes of the planet's clouds.

Jupiter's rapid 10-hour rotation brings features into and out of view in the course of an evening. A feature that rotates into view becomes centered on the planet less than two hours later and has rotated out of view less than two hours after that. In a single (long!) night you can observe the entire planet; during the long nights of winter, you may even see the same feature twice. View the planet early in the evening, and notice that it will present a completely different face 3 hours later. If you are making a sketch, draw the major features first and then fill in the details so as to capture the planet's appearance at a single moment.

Careful observers notice that Jupiter's clouds do not all rotate at the same rate. This is a strange concept to those (like us) who live on a solid planet, where the length of the day is the same everywhere. However, on Jupiter the length of a day depends on the latitude: 9 hours 50 minutes at the equator, and 9 hours 56 minutes at higher latitudes. Over a period of weeks, features near the equator pass those at higher latitudes (as if Cuba moved past Florida), and the clouds at the boundaries become thoroughly mixed.

Jupiter's rapid rotation causes the planet to flatten noticeably at the poles. In fact, the planet's equatorial diameter is 7 percent greater than its polar diameter.

Equally as interesting as its ever-changing clouds are Jupiter's four large moons, called Galilean, as they were discovered in 1609 by Galileo. These moons are so bright they could be seen with the naked eye were they not so close to Jupiter, and generally one or more are visible in steadily held binoculars. People with perfect eyesight sometimes see the outermost moon, Callisto, without optical assistance. Jupiter's handful of much fainter moons are visible only with very large telescopes.

From the earth, we look at Jupiter's equator. Because the planet's moons orbit over its equator, we see the orbits nearly edge-on. They move from one side of Jupiter to the other and in front of and behind the planet, but all the while they remain arrayed in a line.

The four moons orbit Jupiter in "months" whose lengths are 1.8 days for Io, 3.6 days for Europa, 7.2 days for Ganymede, and 16.7 days for Callisto. Io's motion is apparent from hour to hour, and it turns up on the opposite side of the planet as the night before. Callisto's slower orbital motion takes it leisurely from one side of the planet to the other and back again in just over two weeks. When one moon passes near another, you can almost see their relative motion.

Among the easiest planetary events to observe with a small telescope are eclipse phenomena involving Jupiter's moons and their shadows. Like our moon, the moons of Jupiter cast shadows. Jupiter is so huge that, with the exception of outermost Callisto (most of the time), the shadows of its moons fall on the planet once each orbit in an event called a "shadow transit." The shadows slowly creep across the face of Jupiter as a conspicuous dark spot. When a moon itself crosses the face of Jupiter, it passes in front of Jupiter's clouds, but because the moons are so similar in color to the clouds, these transits are surprisingly hard to see. The moons (again usually minus Callisto) are also eclipsed once each orbit when they move into Jupiter's shadow; it is fun to watch a moon disappear into blackness or reappear out of the night sky as it slips into or out of Jupiter's shadow. Plus the moons pass behind Jupiter itself in occultations, disappearing or reappearing from behind the planet's edge.

The times of all these events are printed in major astronomy magazines and can also be found using desktop computer programs, so you can anticipate them and be watching.

The events, which are divided into transits, shadow transits, eclipses, and occultations, are coded this way ("ingress," the initiation of a transit, is the opposite of "egress"): TrI = transit (of the moon) ingress; TrE = transit (of the moon) egress; ShI = transit (of the shadow) ingress; ShE = transit (of the shadow) egress; EcD = eclipse disappearance; EcR = eclipse reappearance; OcD = occultation disappearance; OcR = occultation reappearance. In tables, Jupiter's moons are numbered in order of their distance from the planet: I (Io), II (Europa), III (Ganymede), IV (Callisto). Thus a typical event involving the transit of a shadow across the planet's face might read: "II ShI 4:16, II ShE 7:07," telling you that Europa's shadow begins to move across Jupiter's face at 4:16 and moves off the disk at 7:07. (Remember that times in international publications are usually expressed in Universal Time, which utilizes a 24-hour clock, so be prepared to convert them to your time zone.)

An initial look shows Jupiter's moons to be strung along a line. It is actually slightly more complicated than that. Jupiter—and the plane of its moons—is inclined three degrees to our line of sight, and only twice in its 12-year orbit do we see its equator exactly edge-on. Then, for a period of several months, its moons may eclipse each other in a series of very interesting events. We are in Jupiter's equatorial plane in and around June 2003, April 2009, November 2014, March 2021, and October 2026. Centered around these dates for about two years, Callisto and its shadow can cross Jupiter, whereas normally Callisto and its shadow pass north or south of the planet.

Although Ganymede is the largest moon in the solar system and its three sisters are not much smaller, they are so distant from us that their diameters measure less than two arcseconds. A good telescope on an ideal night for viewing will show them as tiny disks rather than as starlike points, but even then they remain featureless. Rarely has anyone claimed to see surface features on Jupiter's moons. Notice their very subtle color differences, especially when they are next to or in front of the planet.

SATURN

Saturn and our own moon are the two objects that draw the most gasps from people who see them for the first time through a telescope—the moon because of its size and wealth of detail, and Saturn because of its exquisite beauty. Saturn is everybody's favorite planet through a telescope.

It is the rings, of course, that make Saturn so appealing. The planet itself is a sleepy version of Jupiter, with a few relatively featureless dark cloud bands and a white spot now and then. Its rings, however, more than make up for the planet's apparent listlessness.

Saturn's face shows few features. As is true for Jupiter (and Uranus and Neptune), we see but the tops of clouds. Saturn is somewhat smaller and twice as distant as Jupiter, so telescopically it is only about a sixth the area. Saturn is also colder than Jupiter and its atmosphere less active. Plus a high layer of haze masks whatever features might appear. Look for a dark band near the equator and a dark polar area. When Jupiter and Saturn are visible at the same time, notice that Saturn has a softer, creamier appearance than does Jupiter, whose light is harsh in comparison.

Saturn's rapid rotation (10 hours) and low density (less than water) cause the planet to flatten in a polar to equatorial ratio of 9 to 10—this polar flattening is obvious. Also conspicuous (except when the rings are nearly edge-on) are shadows: of the planet on the rings and of the rings on the planet. This latter shadow, which looks like a dark cloud band, is usually the most prominent feature on Saturn. For its part, the shadow of the planet on the rings causes the rings to appear to be cut off on one side where they pass behind the planet. This shadow disappears when Saturn is opposite the sun (at "opposition") and Saturn's shadow falls directly away from the earth; it is most apparent when Saturn is close to being in alignment with the sun. It is then seen to the southeast in the morning sky or to the southwest in the evening sky. The shadow on its rings gives the planet a striking three-dimensional appearance.

Any telescope shows Saturn's rings. The smallest telescopes show what looks like a single ring. A better telescope shows two rings—a broad B ring and a thinner outer A ring—and the dark gap between them known as Cassini's Division. On a night with steady air, look for Saturn's disk shining through Cassini's Division. The best telescopes show a third pale innermost ring called the C, or crepe, ring, which is so transparent the planet may appear to shine through it. They will also reveal that the B ring has a greater brightness than does the narrower and grayer A ring. Encke's Division, which is near the border between the B and C rings, is a challenge to glimpse.

The rings orbit in the same plane as Saturn's equator. The angle at which we see them from the earth varies during Saturn's 30-year orbit, from no inclination (when we see them edge-on) to 27 degrees, when they are displayed in their most open position. When viewed open, the rings extend beyond Saturn's north and south poles and seem to envelop the planet. When edge-on, they briefly disappear in amateur telescopes because of their extreme thinness. The rings are edge-on in September 2009 and March 2025, although Saturn will be behind the sun on those dates and therefore invisible. We will next actually *see* Saturn's rings edge-on in 2038.

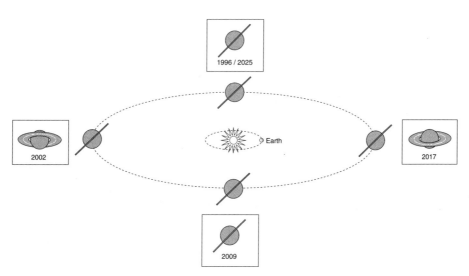

As seen from the earth, Saturn's rings change their orientation as the years pass.

Each year Saturn's rings are in a different aspect than the year before, and this is about the extent of the change you will observe on the planet. Again, ring features are most conspicuous when they are open to our view; they are hard to glimpse when the ring angle is low. Indeed, the rings appear to be a single ring, without division, during the period they are edge-on. Features within them (such as Encke's Division) become progressively more visible as the rings open up and we therefore begin to see them at a more favorable angle.

Saturn is accompanied by an extensive family of moons. In contrast to Jupiter, which has four equally bright moons plus a slew of impossibly faint ones, Saturn has a series of moons displaying different brightnesses. How many you see depends on the size of your telescope. Even good binoculars will show 8th-magnitude Titan, an appropriately named giant with a nitrogen atmosphere even thicker than the earth's. Titan orbits Saturn once every 16 days and can be up to 5 ring diameters east or west of the planet. The other moons take a bit of scrutiny to find with a small telescope, but half a dozen in all can be seen with a large amateur telescope. Rhea, at 10th magnitude, is the second brightest and second easiest to see. Dione and Tethys, magnitudes 10.4 and 10.3, respectively, are similar in their visibility and can be spotted with an 8-inch telescope. Enceladus, 12th magnitude and even closer to the planet, is more of a challenge, while innermost Mimas at 13th magnitude is difficult even with a large telescope, in part because of Saturn's overwhelming glare. Iapetus is an oddity; its two sides have vastly different reflectivity and it varies from magnitude 10 to 12, depending on which of its sides faces the earth.

Saturn's moons change their positions rapidly as they circle the ringed planet, the innermost moons moving noticeably in less than an hour. Monthly astronomy magazines print charts showing where to find its moons relative to the planet.

Twice every Saturn year (twice every 30 Earth years), when the rings are edge-on to the earth, the orbits of the moons are edge-on, too. Then the moons and their shadows transit the face of Saturn and are eclipsed by it. However, the moons are so faint that these interesting events are very difficult to observe in even the best amateur telescopes.

URANUS, NEPTUNE, AND PLUTO

The three outermost planets show no features through a telescope of any size. The most you can do is simply find them! Merely locating Pluto, the farthest distant, requires a large telescope and accurate star chart.

Sixth-magnitude Uranus is barely bright enough to see without optical assistance, even under ideal conditions. Under high magnification, the planet is so large that, despite its great distance, it shows a round disk. This is in fact how it was discovered. Just over two centuries ago, the great amateur astronomer William Herschel was systematically examining each star in the sky under high power when he came across a body that was round. At first he thought he had discovered a distant tailless comet, until its orbit identified it as a giant planet beyond Saturn. A good telescope 4 inches or greater in diameter will show a disk almost 4 arcseconds in diameter, comparable in size to Mars when Mars is at its farthest from the earth. Uranus has an odd blue greenish color caused by methane in its atmosphere.

Neptune, almost twice as distant as Uranus, looks pointlike in a telescope 6 inches or less in diameter. At 8th magnitude, it can be spotted in binoculars. With an apparent diameter of 2 arcseconds, it appears to be the same size as Jupiter's moons, which are closer but proportionately smaller.

The many moons of Uranus and Neptune are visible only with large telescopes. The easiest to see is Neptune's Triton, which is magnitude 13.6 and up to 17 arcseconds from the planet. The brightest moons of Uranus are slightly fainter.

Uranus and Neptune move very slowly against the background of stars and remain in one constellation for several years before moving on. Uranus takes a lifetime, and Neptune two, to move once around the sky, but you can detect their motion week to week against the many faint stars they pass.

Fourteenth magnitude Pluto is beyond the reach of most amateur telescopes. The trick is to identify it in a sky full of faint stars, and detailed star charts are essential.

OCCULTATIONS

On rare occasions, a planet moves in front of a star and occults it. Occultations are listed in annual observers' handbooks and in popular astronomy magazines. Research astronomers can learn much about the structure of a planet's atmosphere by the way starlight fades as it passes through ever deeper layers of the atmosphere. It was through such a stellar occultation that the rings of Uranus were discovered. Amateur astronomers can enjoy the novelty of the event.

Most occultations are over in seconds. However, an occultation of a star by the rings of Saturn is a prolonged event and especially fun to watch as the star seems to slowly "twinkle" as its light passes alternately through thick and thin ring segments. Because of their size and speed, Mars and Jupiter occult more stars than do the other planets.

Occultations of stars by asteroids, timed simultaneously by a team of observers at scattered locations, can provide a profile of the asteroid's shape at that moment and also reveal unknown satellites. Among the more rewarding sights in the sky is the rare passage of a planet in front of (and seemingly through) a star cluster, nebula, or galaxy.

Chapter Seven

✦

OBSERVING ASTEROIDS AND COMETS

Asteroids and comets are minor members of the solar system. Thousands of each are known, and more are discovered every year.

Asteroids are rocky or metallic objects up to a few hundred miles in diameter. Most orbit the sun on relatively circular orbits between Mars and Jupiter in the asteroid belt, although the orbits of many take them to the inner or outer parts of the solar system. A few hundred are known that come close to the earth. Meteorites found in museums are fallen pieces of asteroids. Were an asteroid of significant size to hit our planet, the damage would be catastrophic. Only a few asteroids are bright enough to be seen with binoculars, but dozens can be spotted with a good amateur telescope.

In contrast, comets are made of dirty ice and spend most of their time in the outermost parts of the solar system, far beyond the orbit of Pluto. We see them only when they approach the sun. They appear unexpectedly (with a few exceptions), are bright for a few weeks or months, and then suddenly disappear. A bright comet is one of the most unusual sights in a dark sky, and formerly the appearance of comets caused widespread panic.

ASTEROIDS

What's fun about asteroids is finding them; there is not much to see once you have located one. Even the largest look like stars through the largest telescopes (hence their name, which means "starlike" in Greek). Vesta is bright enough to see with the naked eye, and several can be seen with binoculars; dozens are within range of a good amateur telescope. Asteroids move night to night against the stars as they orbit the sun, and the challenge is to plot them on a good star chart and then pinpoint their location. The thrill is in the hunt and in adding to your list of conquests.

Asteroids occasionally pass in front of a star, eclipsing it for a mere few seconds. Serious amateur astronomers record the precise times of such events to help increase our knowledge of asteroid diameters and positions. The timing of asteroid eclipses in fact remains an area where amateur astronomers with modest equipment (essentially a telescope and standard video camera) can make scientific contributions. The International Occultation Timing Association (c/o Rex Easton; 2007 S.W. Mission Ave., Apt. 1; Topeka, KS, 66604-3341; skygazer@smartnet.net) coordinates amateur observations.

Most asteroids are irregular in shape and change their brightnesses as they rotate. Several vary in magnitude by enough to notice in a few hours.

Asteroids occasionally pass in front of star clusters, nebulae, and galaxies. Although of no scientific value, such events are fun to watch.

COMETS

All asteroids look basically the same except for brightness, and none do anything unexpected. Every comet, on the other hand, is different, and its behavior cannot be predicted. Most, however, are very faint and require some skill merely to locate.

Comets generally travel on highly elongated orbits that bring them from the outer reaches of the solar system, where they spend most of their time, to the region of the inner planets. There they warm up and become bright enough to see. A comet is visible only relatively briefly; seeming to appear out of nowhere, comets visit a short while and then disappear into the depths of space.

Each year, about two dozen new comets are discovered and a few known ones return. While most are visible only with professional telescopes, a few come within range of amateur equipment. As with asteroids, the challenge with faint comets is in finding them. They appear as tiny fuzzy patches of light. Although they might brighten unexpectedly or develop some structure, faint comets are seldom exciting objects.

Bright comets are rare, and with the single exception of Halley's, they appear unexpectedly. The next bright comet we *know* will appear is in fact Halley's when it returns in

2134. (On its return in 2061, Halley's Comet will be poorly positioned and therefore disappointing to view.) Many bright comets will grace our skies before then, but all will be discovered only months to a year in advance of their greatest brilliance. A "great comet," like 1997's Hale-Bopp, passes by once every 20 years or so.

The best way to know about the discovery of new comets is to subscribe to an electronic mail astronomy news bulletin service or to regularly check one of the many Internet sites devoted to comets. By the time you hear about a comet in an astronomy magazine, it is old news.

A bright comet is thrilling to watch because it has structure. Also, comets appear to evolve. As a general rule (the sun and planets are the only major exceptions), astronomical objects do not change. The Orion Nebula looks the same now as it did ten thousand years ago. Comets, however, change weekly, often in unpredictable ways.

A comet has three main parts. The *nucleus* is the solid, durable part that returns time and time again. It is essentially a chunk of frozen ices (largely water ice and frozen carbon dioxide, or "dry ice") with silicate grains mixed in. A typical nucleus is merely a mile or so in diameter—far too small to be seen if the comet remained frozen. As the comet approaches the sun, however, the ices warm up. They then evaporate and shoot out of cracks in the crust as jets of gas and dust to form a huge cloud surrounding the nucleus. Called the *head,* this cloud is far larger than the earth. Sunlight causes the gas in it to glow as gas does in a fluorescent tube, while the dust particles reflect the sun's light. A stream of electrified particles from the sun called the "solar wind" blows through the solar system and, catching the gas and dust in the comet's head, throws them back to form the *tail.* The tail points away from the sun; its orientation tells you the direction to the sun, though not the direction the comet is traveling. Bright comets have two tails: a gas tail made of electrified, glowing gas (or ions) and a dust tail made of dust particles that reflect sunlight. The dust tail is generally much broader and brighter. Tails of major comets contain so few particles that they are a nearly perfect vacuum, and we see them only because they are so huge: a comet's tail can stretch from one planet to another. Although amazingly beautiful, this tail is all show and little substance. A comet's tail is indeed "closer to nothing than anything can be and still be something."

To review: Tails originate from gas jetted out through cracks in the crust of the nucleus. This flow of material can alter from day to day as the comet warms and rotates. The tail therefore can change quite unpredictably. In extreme cases, the nucleus can even split apart.

Because comets are nebulous objects with low surface brightnesses, only their brighter parts are visible under an urban sky. Most of the tail is no brighter than the Milky Way, and the sky must be dark to see its full extent. People who watch a comet from the city see only the innermost part of its tail while its bulk, including all its fine structure, is lost. The rule of thumb is that if you cannot see the Milky Way, you cannot see a comet's tail. Comet Hale-Bopp was an exception; it was so bright that the first few degrees of its tail could be seen even from a city ablaze with light. Most of the comet's long and beautiful tail, however, could not.

When examining a comet through binoculars or a telescope, look for delicate structure in the head and tail. Buried deep inside the head, the nucleus itself is too small to see, but can you spot the bright nuclear area? What shape does it have? Do you notice how the gas jets out of the nucleus? The rotating nucleus often appears to be tumbling erratically causing material to spray in a complex pattern. The solar wind blowing this material back sometimes creates shock waves or a bow shock. Notice how material is not

Most comets have short tails, but the tail of a bright comet can stretch across much of the sky. 1996 Comet Hyakutake. Photograph by Bruce M. Gottlieb.

expelled evenly—it often ejects in spurts, and knots of material may travel from the head down the tail. Comets can even break apart (a spectacular example being Shoemaker-Levy 9, which smacked into Jupiter in 1994). Look for color in the tail or tails; yellow is generally reflected sunlight while blue is fluorescing gas. How long and how wide is the tail? How does it curve? Gas tails are straighter than dust tails. An "antitail" looks like a tail pointing the wrong way, toward the sun, but it is actually a plane of gas that, from our viewing angle, projects in front of the comet. Sketching what you see will improve your powers of observation. Remember: Bright comets are newly discovered; because they have not been observed before, no one can predict their behavior. We will all discover together how they behave.

If a comet passes fairly close to the earth, watch for it to change position daily, moving from one constellation to another in a few days and even crossing the entire sky in a few weeks. Not only can a comet change its *appearance* relatively quickly, but it can change its *position* quickly, too.

Comets that orbit the sun in periods of a century or less have already been identified, but comets that come our way only once every thousands of years are still being discovered. Although few professional astronomers search for new comets, it remains a popular activity for advanced amateurs. Indeed, amateur comet hunters outnumber the professionals, discovering a disproportionate amount of bright new comets. A powerful incentive is that, unlike any other object in the sky, a comet is named for its discoverer (or codiscoverers), and identifying a major new comet is a route to instant—if perhaps short-lived—fame, as Alan Hale and Thomas Bopp will attest.

Chapter Eight

✦

OBSERVING METEORS

Most meteors originate from comets, although they look nothing like them. A meteor (also called a shooting or falling star) is the flash of light produced when a particle of dust shed long ago by a comet falls through our atmosphere and bursts into flame. The dust particles fall so fast—typically at speeds of 100,000 miles per hour—that friction with the air causes them to burn up, even though they are made of silicate materials normally considered fireproof. Meteors from comets generally do not survive their fall toward the ground.

Some meteors come from asteroids; these objects are chunks of solid silicates or iron. They are structurally strong enough to survive their fiery plunge through the atmosphere. If they reach the ground, they are called meteorites.

Meteors are generally made by particles no larger than a grain of sand. How can such a tiny object generate so bright a light? The truth is, meteors reach temperatures of 4,000 degrees Fahrenheit—as hot as a welding torch—and appear against a very dark background. After all, a star is not very bright either, but you can see it at night.

Cosmic debris the size of a marble or pea causes an especially bright meteor, leaving people to gasp in astonishment. Debris the size of a football produces a spectacularly brilliant meteor called a fireball (more rarely called a bolide, to use an obscure term). A fireball can light up the sky like the full moon. These meteors often end in explosions. Large bits of cosmic debris can also reach the ground—if the size, say, of an office building, the debris can explode on impact and blast out a crater.

People often assume that the fireball they saw eventually landed in a nearby field, whereas in reality it streaked far beyond the horizon and probably burst in the air. Meteors

A meteor captured on film during the annual Perseid Meteor Shower. (Background stars produced short streaks during the time exposure.) Photograph by Bruce M. Gottlieb.

flame at heights of dozens of miles and often travel from one state to another. A meteor coming toward you would appear to be a stationary burst of light. In fact, all except giant meteors slow down enough to stop burning at a height of more than 40 miles and fall the rest of the way to the earth in darkness and silence.

The brightest meteors leave smoke trains or trails, which last from seconds to an hour or more. Smoke trails are fun to watch in binoculars.

Technically, a *meteor* is the flash of light produced by a falling *meteorite*. The meteorite is the solid object; the meteor is the visible phenomenon. The older term *meteoroid* refers to the meteorite in space, before it enters the atmosphere.

On a typical dark night, a single observer will see an average of seven meteors an hour, with three times as many falling in the predawn hours as during the evening. They appear at random over the sky. Most meteors are faint, but many are visible through a telescope. A few hundred thousand visible meteors appear every night somewhere over the earth.

Advertisements in the major astronomy magazines offer to sell meteorites to collectors and to anyone who would like to own something originating in outer space.

METEOR SHOWERS

Several times a year, meteors fall in much greater numbers than average and we experience a "meteor shower." There are actually dozens of showers each year, but most are sparse and are of interest only to specialists. The best showers, when meteors fall at the rate of almost one a minute, are tremendously exciting, and some people plan their vacations around them. The Perseid Meteor Shower, which peaks on or near August 12, is the most popular, because it falls during the summer months when people enjoy staying outside late. However, the Geminids display in December is equally rich.

A meteor shower happens when the earth crosses the orbit of an active comet and passes through a swarm of debris shed by the comet long ago. This debris is in orbit around the sun, and because the earth passes through it at the same time each year when our two orbits intersect, showers are fairly predictable. Just as raindrops or snowflakes appear to emanate from a radiant point when you drive through a rain or snowstorm, meteors in a shower seem to radiate from a certain point in the sky as the earth moves through them. The shower is named after the constellation from which the meteors appear to radiate (the Perseid meteors, for example, radiate from Perseus. The *id* suffix to the shower's name means "of" or "from" in Greek). More meteors are visible after the radiant point rises, which for most showers is after midnight. Although some meteors fall during the evening, prime meteor time is generally the wee hours of the morning.

If you are planning to watch meteors long into the night, it is important to make yourself comfortable (and warm in cooler months). Lawn chairs are popular meteor-observing accessories, as are sleeping bags (although they can be *too* comfortable late at night), and snacks and warm drinks are generally considered essential. Serious observers plot the meteors they see on sky maps, often noting timing data verbally into a tape recorder, information that contributes greatly to our understanding of the distribution of comet particles in space. Here's a fairly simple way to make a scientific contribution if coordinated with a national or international organization. Meteor observation remains primarily the domain of dedicated amateur astronomers.

Meteors are surprisingly easy to photograph. Set a camera on a tripod pointing upward, and take time exposures of up to 20 minutes duration (depending on lens, film, and sky brightness). The stars will form short trails unless your camera is on a clockdriven mount that compensates for the earth's rotation. Be prepared to throw away most of the exposures, but bright meteors that happen to pass by while your shutter is open will photograph nicely.

MAJOR METEOR SHOWERS

date	name	constellation	max / hr
January 3	Quadrantids	Boötes	60
May 5	Eta Aquarids	Aquarius	20
July 28	Delta Aquarids	Aquarius	10
August 12	Perseids	Perseus	70
October 21	Orionids	Orion	10
November 17	Leonids	Leo	variable
December 13	Geminids	Gemini	60

Showers peak within a day or two of the dates listed here. The "max/hr" is the maximum number of meteors a person might see in one hour under ideal conditions. Bright moonlight often interferes.

Dozens of minor meteors showers are known but poorly charted. Amateurs can contribute to scientific knowledge by observing meteors systematically on standardized forms and reporting the results to a central authority. No telescope is required, but patience is essential.

PART III: THE STARS AND BEYOND

Chapter Nine

OBSERVING DOUBLE AND VARIABLE STARS

All stars are not equal. The most obvious difference is their apparent brightness. Although the brightness we see tells us nothing about a star's true, intrinsic brightness (for which we need to know its distance), it does allow us to express how bright the star appears in our sky. Brightnesses are expressed by the magnitude system, developed over 2,000 years ago.

A star's name is also useful information. The brightest handful of stars are given letters of the Greek alphabet; others are assigned catalog numbers. Only a few dozen, like Arcturus, have proper names. Those without names are known by their coordinates on the sky. Nonstellar objects like star clusters and galaxies have catalog numbers.

✦ GREEK ALPHABET ✦

The brightest stars are named with letters of the Greek alphabet, followed by the Latin possessive form of the constellation in which they appear. Usually the brightest star in a constellation is named Alpha. For example, Vega is known as Alpha in Lyra (or Alpha Lyrae for short).

$$\alpha \; \beta \; \gamma \; \delta \; \epsilon \; \zeta \; \eta \; \theta \; \iota \; \kappa \; \lambda \; \mu \; \nu \; \xi \; o \; \pi \; \rho \; \sigma \; \tau \; \upsilon \; \phi \; \chi \; \psi \; \omega$$

✦ MAGNITUDE SYSTEM ✦

Since the time of Hipparchus in the second century B.C., stars have been ranked by brightness according to their magnitude. *The magnitude of a star expresses its apparent brightness as seen from the earth but tells us nothing about the star's intrinsic luminosity. Hipparchus divided all naked-eye stars into 6 magnitudes, assigning a magnitude of 1 to the brightest and 6 to the faintest. His system has since been put on a firm mathematical footing and extended to both brighter and fainter objects. The very brightest objects have negative magnitudes (Sirius is magnitude −1.5; the full moon, −12). The faintest stars visible from a city are magnitude 4 or 5; on a clear moonless night, 6; with binoculars or a small telescope, 9; with a good amateur telescope, about 14; and with the Hubble Space Telescope, 30. The progression from one magnitude to the next represents a change of 2.5 times (a 3rd magnitude star is 2.5 times brighter than a 4th magnitude star), so that a 1st magnitude star is 100 times brighter than one of 6th magnitude.*

Solitary stars are not much to look at unless they display some color. Most stars are white, but a few bright stars have enough color to trigger sensors in your eye to then appear tinted. The hottest stars, such as Rigel, Deneb, and Vega, are blue white. Cooler stars like Arcturus are yellow. The coolest giant stars, like Antares, Betelgeuse, and Arcturus, are called red but in reality appear yellowish orange. A telescope enhances the color. Be aware, however, that inexpensive refracting telescopes lacking color-corrected lenses create false colors, as does atmospheric twinkling.

DOUBLE STARS

Many amateurs enjoy hunting down and observing *double stars*. Double stars are two stars that appear close together. They may actually be in orbit around each other, in which case they are a *binary star system* (physically connected by gravity), or they may only appear to be close, when in reality one lies far beyond the other. Such false pairs are called "optical doubles." True binary stars complete an orbit in a few years to many thousands of years. Although orbital motion cannot be watched directly because it is so slow, it can be measured as the years pass.

The thrill in observing double stars lies in their beauty, especially when colors contrast (good examples are Albireo in Cygnus and Gamma Andromedae), and in the challenge of locating them. Pairs composed of widely separated bright stars are easy to see as distinct objects. More often, one star is much fainter than its companion or the two are very close together, and then it takes some skill and optical excellence to see both. There is always the wonder of what we are seeing: Two remote suns born together and locked in an eternal gravitational embrace. Groups of three or even four stars, collectively called a *multiple star system,* are occasionally found.

Double stars are characterized by the magnitudes of the two stars and the angular distance between them. Distances are expressed in arcseconds, one arcsecond being ⅟₆₀ of ⅟₆₀ of a degree. Observers quickly learn the *resolving power* of their telescope—the telescope's ability to separate close objects. The resolving power of the human eye is about 200 arcseconds, of a 2-inch refracting telescope not quite 2 arcseconds, and of a 200-inch telescope perhaps ¼ arcsecond in actual practice. Large telescopes do not perform spectacularly better than small telescopes, because they are limited by the blurring effects of atmospheric turbulence. Observers of double stars need a night of calm air ("good seeing") and often use very high magnification. The *position angle* expresses the direction of the companion from the primary star. Both the separation and position angles change as the stars complete their orbit.

Double Star Polaris. Photograph by Jack Schmidling.

Observing two stars that are close together is easier when they are of equal brightness than when one is much brighter than the other. The classic example involves Sirius. Its 8th-magnitude companion would be easily visible with the cheapest binoculars except that it is so close to Sirius it is overwhelmed—lost in the glare of this star's −1.4 magnitude—and so remains a challenge to see even in a large telescope. Double stars come in every conceivable ratio of brightnesses and distances, and no two pairs are identical.

Other than the fun of tracking them down, little else involving binary stars is available to the amateur astronomer. A niche pursuit is to measure their positions with a filar micrometer eyepiece, although this essentially 19th century activity is no longer in vogue.

Nevertheless, hundreds of double stars are visible in amateur telescopes, and a person can keep busy for years tracking them all down. The more interesting systems are described in this book.

✦ LIGHT YEAR ✦

Distances beyond our solar system are expressed in light years. *One light year is simply the distance that light travels in a year. A unit of* distance, *not* time, *it is equal to almost 6 trillion miles, or 63,240 times the distance from the earth to the sun. To put this in perspective, if the 93 million miles from the earth to the sun were represented by 1 inch, 1 light year would be 1 mile.*

VARIABLE STARS

Happily for us, our sun shines with a constant light. Some stars are unstable, however, and their brightnesses fluctuate erratically. Other stars eclipse each other rhythmically, dimming briefly when one blocks the other. A few erupt unexpectedly and some explode. Stars vary their brightness in a bewildering variety of ways, and there are dozens of classes of variable stars. Studying them constitutes an entire branch of astronomy.

Determining how unstable stars alter their brightness tells us about the conditions within stars during stages of their evolution. Some variable stars (the Cepheids) provide information vital to determining distances to far-away star clusters and galaxies. The only way to determine how a star changes its brightness is to watch it closely for a long period of time—a laborious activity.

Tens of thousands of variable stars are cataloged—far too many for the handful of professional astronomers who study them to monitor more than a fraction. That is why variable-star observation is one activity in which amateurs have made major contributions to astronomy. In former times, amateurs made brightness estimates by visually comparing the target variable with nearby stars of known and constant brightness; today, electronic cameras attached to computers have automated the process.

The most cataclysmic variable stars are *supernovae*—stars that unexpectedly explode. A formerly faint star can become one of the brightest stars in the sky, or at least in the galaxy where it resides. Supernovae cannot be predicted but nevertheless need to be studied as soon as they explode, so a popular amateur activity is to monitor distant galaxies and strike the alarm when an explosion occurs. Supernova searches are currently carried out by teams of amateurs outfitted with large telescopes and electronic cameras. A related activity is searching for *novae*—stars that flare suddenly, then gradually return to their former brightness. Novae occur all throughout the sky (with a concentration toward the Milky Way), so it is hard to search for them systematically. Some amateurs visually memorize a small section of the sky and scan it nightly for "new" stars that appear.

A handful of variable stars are so conspicuous they can be followed with binoculars or even the naked eye. They are described in this book (Delta in Cepheus, Mira in Cetus, and Algol in Perseus). If you succumb to the allure of monitoring them, contact the American Association of Variable Star Observers (25 Birch Street, Cambridge, MA 02138-1205; (617) 354-0484). The AAVSO coordinates amateur activities in North America, and its work is highly respected by the community of professional astronomers.

✦ A NOTE ON NUMBERS ✦

Surprisingly, many of the fundamental facts in astronomy are insufficiently known. Beyond our solar system, distances, luminosities, diameters, ages, and even magnitudes are based on measurements that are difficult to make precisely and are often no better than educated guesses. Don't be surprised if the distance to a well-known bright star is listed as 250 light years in one book and 1,100 in another—the truth is, no one knows for sure. Only the most recent data is used in this book, but it too is subject to revision as our tools and techniques continue to improve.

✳

Chapter Ten

OBSERVING STAR CLUSTERS, NEBULAE, AND GALAXIES

Our own galaxy, the Milky Way, is the largest visible structure in the sky. Fortunately, it can be enjoyed without a telescope. It comprises countless individual stars, along with *star clusters* and giant clouds of gas called *nebulae*, among other objects. Beyond are distant galaxies; many can be spotted in small telescopes and are therefore popular with amateur astronomers. Collectively, these are called *deep-space objects*.

For the same reason the Milky Way appears to best advantage in a dark sky, star clusters and especially nebulae and galaxies require darkness to be seen: Such objects, having a low surface brightness, show up only when they contrast against a dark background. Only a handful of the brightest can be viewed from within a city, and even then not well. It seems to be an inescapable fact that most of the spectacular things in the sky cannot be seen from where most people live; astronomy often obliges you to travel to where it can be practiced best.

Deep-space objects are invariably faint. The rule is, the bigger the telescope, the better (other things being equal). The goal is to gather as much light as possible to increase the brightness of what initially appears faint. Low-power eyepieces give the widest views. It is certainly ironic that owners of large telescopes buy expensive eyepieces to make them as *low* power as possible, but the truth is, a large telescope operating on low magnification gives the best views of most deep-space objects. Small planetary nebulae and globular star clusters, however, will withstand high powers.

Deep-space objects are generally known by their designations in two popular catalogs. The most famous was devised by Charles Messier, a comet hunter in the late part of the 18th century, whose Messier Catalog contains 109 relatively bright objects widely known by their "M" number. Many amateurs have seen all 109. A century later, Charles Dryer completed his New General Catalog (later supplemented by two Index Catalogs) of 13,226 deep-space objects known by their NGC and IC numbers. The comparatively brief Messier Catalog is printed in its entirety in many popular astronomy books; the NGC and IC catalogs fill a large volume available from Sky Publishing Corporation.

STAR CLUSTERS

People are (usually) born one at a time, but stars are born in large groups called star clusters. Many clusters dissipate relatively quickly, and the member stars go their separate ways. This happened to the cluster, long since "evaporated," where our own sun was born. Nevertheless, many star clusters remain.

If the stars comprising the cluster are not tightly packed but instead have a loose or "open" relationship with one another, they form an *open cluster*. Open star clusters contain anywhere from dozens to thousands of member stars. Rarely does one have a definite shape; rather, they are amorphous collections of both bright and faint stars. Open clusters are usually found within the limits of the Milky Way, and for that reason they are sometimes called "galactic clusters." Constellations that lie along the Milky Way, like Perseus and Cygnus, are rich in open clusters, while constellations far from the Milky Way, like Leo and Pisces, have few.

All the stars in a single open cluster are the same age. We see both young and old open clusters, their appearance changing as they age. Young clusters have brilliant, hot blue giant stars that burn out quickly, astronomically speaking, while the brightest stars of old clusters are aged giants, yellow and red and quite different in structure. The study of open clusters has been vital to unraveling the story of how stars evolve as they grow old and eventually die.

Open clusters that are visible without a telescope include the Pleiades and Hyades in Taurus, the Beehive in Cancer, the Perseus Double Cluster, and the entire constellation Coma Berenices. The Ursa Major Moving Group, which includes most of the stars of the Big Dipper and a few others nearby, is so close and so open that it cannot be recognized as a single structure without plotting the stars' motions. A few dozen distant clusters are visible in binoculars, and more than a hundred can be spotted in a small telescope.

Open star cluster M37. Photograph by Rockett Crawford.

The second type of star cluster is far more compact and symmetrical. These clusters form huge spheres or globes and are called *globular* (pronounced "**glob**-u-lar") clusters. They are invariably larger than open clusters (up to a few hundred light years in diameter) and contain many more stars (perhaps a million). Their luminosity is about 100,000 times that of our sun, but none are as close to us or as bright as the most visible open star clusters, and all require a decent telescope to appreciate. To the nonspecialist, they all look alike except for size and brightness, but on closer inspection, they are also seen to vary in the amount of stars concentrated toward the center. All globular clusters are distant, and through a small telescope, they look like tiny balls of hazy light. Through a larger telescope, these remarkable objects reveal themselves to be made up of countless stars.

Most open clusters are quite young, and some have just finished forming. In contrast, globular clusters are among the oldest structures in the Milky Way. They consist of aged yellow stars. Because of their great age, globular clusters are important to our understanding of the history of galaxies.

Globular star cluster M22. Photograph by Jack Schmidling.

Globular clusters are distributed symmetrically around the center of the Milky Way. Most are concentrated in Sagittarius, Scorpius, and nearby constellations. A few hundred are known in our galaxy, and amateur astronomers with good telescopes can see a few dozen of the brightest. The two best for Northern Hemisphere observers are M13 in Hercules and M22 in Sagittarius.

BRIGHT NEBULAE

Roughly a tenth of the material in our Milky Way has not yet formed into stars, remaining as immense clouds of gas called *nebulae.* Most of this gas is hydrogen and most of the rest helium, with small amounts of other elements mixed in.

A nebula cannot be seen unless it is illuminated. Otherwise, it blocks the light of stars behind it and appears to be a dark "hole" in the Milky Way. Examples include the Pipe Nebula in Ophiuchus and the lane dividing M42 and M43 in Orion. Countless dark nebulae show up on long-time-exposure photographs, but few are visible to the eye.

Bright nebulae, not surprisingly, are far more interesting. They are lit by hot young stars that have recently formed within them. Rather than reflecting starlight directly, these nebulae glow as does the gas in a fluorescent tube; for this reason they are also called "emission nebulae." Ultraviolet radiation from hot stars ionizes nearby hydrogen gas; this radiation strips protons from hydrogen atoms to produce free-ranging protons and electrons. When recaptured by a proton to form another hydrogen atom, the electron radiates light at frequencies that give a nebula its characteristic red and green colors. Additional ultraviolet light soon knocks the electron loose again, after which it is captured by another proton, and the cycle repeats. The net result is that ultraviolet light radiated by hot stars causes a nearby cloud of hydrogen gas to glow.

Bright nebulae are delicate and exquisitely diffuse structures that require the darkest of moonless skies to fully appreciate. Small telescopes show only their brighter central portions; large telescopes reveal the fainter outlying regions.

The best bright nebulae to view are, in winter, the Great Nebula in Orion and, in summer, the Trifid, Lagoon, and Omega Nebulae in Sagittarius. Special but expensive "nebular filters" attached to eyepieces increase contrast and make nebulae much easier to see.

Two nebula described in this book (M78 in Orion and part of M20 in Sagittarius) are *reflection nebulae*. Unlike emission nebulae, which shine by fluorescence and produce their own light, reflection nebulae merely reflect starlight from nearby bright stars. Hot stars are bluish and so are reflection nebulae (although the subtle color is seen only in time-exposure color photographs).

The Orion Nebula. Photograph by Bruce M. Gottlieb.

PLANETARY NEBULAE

Diffuse nebulae are where stars are being born; planetary nebulae are where stars are dying.

"Planetaries," as they are called, are shells of gas expelled by unstable stars approaching the ends of their lives. The stars jettison their outer layers in a series of relatively gentle explosions, and these layers expand into space until they dissipate and fade from view thousands of years later. Having lost its outer layers, the very hot core of the once active star shines at the nebula's center until it cools and fades. These star cores—now dying white dwarfs not much larger than the earth—are among the hottest stars of all, with temperatures approaching 200,000 degrees Fahrenheit. All planetaries have a central star, but most are too faint for amateur telescopes. The hot star illuminates the nebula with intense ultraviolet light and causes it to fluoresce. Many planetaries have a greenish color (visible only with larger telescopes), produced by ionized oxygen. Planetaries are generally smaller than one light year in diameter; by the time they expand to a larger size, they become too diffuse to see, and after a few tens of thousands of years, they dissipate and disappear. Because they are so small, view them with medium and high magnifications.

Planetaries give us a preview of our own future. Our sun is expected to expel a planetary nebula in about 6 billion years.

The term "planetary nebula" reflects the ignorance of an earlier age. William Herschel, the discoverer of the planet Uranus, compared these small round greenish nebulae to the disk of the planet he had recently discovered. However, they have nothing to do with planets.

A few planetaries (the Crab Nebula in Taurus being the prime example) represent the catastrophic deaths of stars that exploded. They are more correctly called *supernova*

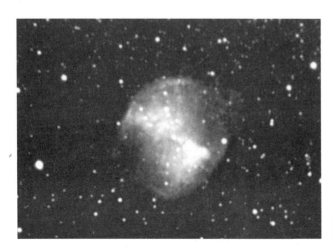

Planetary nebula M27.
Photograph by Jack Schmidling.

remnants to distinguish them from the far more gentle events that create most planetary nebulae.

Planetary nebulae are responsible for enriching with heavy elements the gas that lies between stars. Originally the universe consisted only of hydrogen and helium. Common elements such as carbon and nitrogen are created in giant stars and spread through space when these stars expel their outer layers. The next generation of stars is born from this enriched mixture. The new heavy elements make it possible for planets like the earth to form and eventually for life to evolve—and to figure out how the elements first came to be!

The brightest planetary nebula is the Dumbbell Nebula M27 in Vulpecula; the most famous is the nearby Ring Nebula M57 in Lyra. The Dumbbell is the only planetary visible with binoculars.

GALAXIES

All the stars we see in the night sky are part of our Milky Way. Beyond it lie countless millions of other galaxies, each made up of billions of stars. Although unimaginably enormous in size, their great distances reduce them to small fuzzy patches of light as seen through a telescope. Popular objects for amateurs under a dark sky, hundreds are visible even in a modest telescope.

Galaxies come in a variety of shapes and sizes. Our Milky Way is a large spiral, perhaps with a bar spanning its center (we call it the Milky Way Bar). We cannot see our own galaxy's spiral shape from our position inside it, but we can see other spiral galaxies. Their spiral shape can be discerned, however, only in large telescopes; in small telescopes, all galaxies appear to be formless smudges. Spiral galaxies have spiral arms that coil around a bright center. Elliptical galaxies are more symmetrical; some are huge spheres of stars. Dustless, they lack the interesting shapes of spirals. While some are truly gigantic, more common are dwarf ellipticals. Because of their low surface brightness, dwarfs are maddeningly hard to see, even if they are relatively close by. Galaxies that are irregular in shape are unimaginatively called irregular galaxies. Galaxies are observed at all conceivable orientations, and to the keen eye, no two look alike.

Our Milky Way is one of the largest galaxies known, having a diameter of over 100,000 light years and containing several hundred billion stars. The largest galaxies—giant ellipticals—are perhaps ten times greater in diameter than our own and encompass trillions of stars; the smallest seem to be no more than intergalactic globular clusters.

Spiral Galaxy M101. Photograph by Jack Schmidling.

Through a small telescope, expect even the brightest galaxies to look like small, indistinct smudges. You will see little beyond their overall shape and the amount of central concentration. Galaxies are among the more unremarkable deep-space objects seen through small telescopes, and often the only reward they provide is the satisfaction of finding them. Here is where imagination is important: in turning a faint smudge into a system of hundreds of billions of stars millions of light years away. Only with a telescope 6 inches or larger do you see hints of structure in the brightest galaxies. The largest amateur telescopes show the spiral structures of the closest spirals, dust lanes in edge-on spirals, bright concentrations of gas and stars within galaxies, and dwarf galaxies. In all cases, a dark, moonless night is essential.

The distribution of galaxies in the sky is opposite to the distribution of open star clusters and nebulae. Most star clusters and nebulae are found within the boundaries of the Milky Way. However, we cannot see through our own galaxy to galaxies that lie on its far side, so none appear in or near the Milky Way. Galaxies are found only where we can see far into space, which is away from the direction of our own Milky Way. Good galaxy hunting awaits in Leo, Virgo, and Ursa Major.

Two galaxies bright enough to see without a telescope are the Andromeda Galaxy in Andromeda and M33 in nearby Triangulum. (Two even brighter galaxies, the Large and Small Magellanic Clouds, are visible from the Southern Hemisphere.) Despite their relative closeness, even these large spirals have no apparent shape without the use of a large amateur telescope.

Galaxies are not distributed randomly through space. They tend to cluster. Our Milky Way is one of the largest members in a group of more than two dozen galaxies, most of them very small, which is officially (and affectionately) called the Local Group. The nearest large cluster of galaxies to the Local Group is the Virgo Cluster of Galaxies, found in the constellations Virgo and Leo. It is most visible in the spring. Of the two or so thousand galaxies in this cluster, which lie about 60 million light years from Earth, the few dozen brighter members are visible in good amateur telescopes. Other, fainter clusters of galaxies are within the reach of large amateur instruments.

The most distant object visible in a large amateur telescope is the quasar 3C 273. A quasar is a bright, active center of a galaxy (the surrounding galaxy is generally invisible), and it appears starlike. Thirteenth-magnitude 3C 273 is more than 2 billion light years distant in Virgo.

Some amateur astronomers enjoy hunting within distant galaxies for exploding stars called supernovae. Because there are too many galaxies for professional astronomers to monitor continuously, amateurs can make a contribution to science by systematically scanning for new ones and reporting those they discover.

Chapter Eleven

∵✦∴

OBJECTS FOR BINOCULARS
AND TELESCOPES
BY CONSTELLATION

The trick in observing deep-space objects is simply to *find* them. No other activity challenges novice observers more than finding their way around the nooks and crannies of the sky. It is a skill that can be learned easily enough, but as is true for so many tasks, the proper tools are essential. The essential tool here is a star atlas.

There is not enough space in this slim book to print a proper atlas of the sky. The charts provided here will help you to locate the brighter objects, but any traveler to a strange land knows the value of a detailed map. One or more of the following inexpensive star atlases will make a very useful companion to this book (all are available from Sky Publishing Corp., the parent of *Sky & Telescope* magazine).

Bright Star Atlas 2000.0: This very basic black-and-white atlas shows stars to magnitude 6.5 on 10 charts, each 9 × 12 inches, accompanied by a list of the 600 brightest deep-space objects. 32 pages.

Sky Atlas for Small Telescopes and Binoculars: Eight simple charts show the entire sky to 6th magnitude. Almost 200 deep-space objects are plotted and described, and some are shown on close-up charts of selected regions.

Edmund Mag 6 Star Atlas: Perhaps the best beginner star atlas. Inexpensive, it shows the sky to magnitude 6.2 in 12 oversize charts, each 12 inches square, with three additional close-ups of Orion, the Virgo galaxies, and the Sagittarius area. It lists over a thousand double and variable stars and deep-space objects and has sections on getting started in amateur astronomy. Inexpensive. 68 pages.

Norton's 2000.0 Star Atlas and Reference Handbook: The granddaddy of popular star atlases, Norton's remains popular despite its dated appearance. Eighteen charts show stars to magnitude 6.5, while tables list interesting objects. 179 pages.

Cambridge Star Atlas: Twenty charts show stars to magnitude 6.5, plus 900 deep-space objects. Tables list data for each object. Moon map provided. 90 pages.

Sky Atlas 2000.0: This standard reference is the only atlas that observers with small telescopes will need. Twenty-six folding charts, each 18 × 13½ inches, show stars to magnitude 8 as well as 2,500 deep-space objects. Charts only—no tables or descriptions. 26 charts.

See Chapter 13, "Where to Go From Here" for additional suggestions.

All objects listed by constellation are visible in a 3-inch telescope, and many are visible (though barely) in binoculars. In this book, a *small telescope* is defined as a refractor 4 inches in diameter or less or a reflector up to 6 inches in diameter, a *large telescope* is a reflector in the 8- to 13-inch range, and *largest telescope* refers to an instrument 16 inches or more in diameter.

THE CONSTELLATIONS

ANDROMEDA—Princess Andromeda (an-drom-eh-da)
(chart 2)

Double Star Gamma Andromedae: Andromeda's left foot is one of the most beautiful and colorful double stars in the sky in telescopes of all sizes. It is notable for the dramatic color contrast between the brighter 2.2-magnitude yellow-orange star and its 4.9-magnitude bluish companion 10 arcseconds distant. Use low power. At a recorded distance of 120 light years, the stars are, respectively, 90 and 15 times the luminosity of our sun. Their orbital period is too long to measure.

Planetary Nebula NGC 7662: Nicknamed the Blue Snowball, this 9th-magnitude nebula appears as a small blue dot in a small telescope and a ring in a larger scope. It is 4,000 light years distant and ½ light year in diameter (or 20 arcseconds, measured visually).

"Andromeda Galaxy" M31: The Andromeda Galaxy is the brightest and best known galaxy in the northern sky (other than our own Milky Way). A 5th-magnitude splotch of light, it is barely visible without a telescope but is easy to see in binoculars. Through a small telescope, it is a bright but essentially shapeless glob of light without clearly defined boundaries; a larger telescope (or darker night) reveals its elliptical shape. A spiral similar to our own, we see it oriented merely 12 degrees from edge-on. We see only the innermost, brightest part of it, which appears nearly as large as our moon. Its outer regions extend to a distance of 3 degrees from the center, but these dim regions, which show up well on time-exposure photographs, are difficult to see otherwise. The Andromeda Galaxy, a system of hundreds of billions of stars about 2,900,000,000 light years away, is famous as the most distant object you can see with your eyes alone. Our Milky Way would look similar if viewed from the Andromeda Galaxy. Edwin Hubble's discovery of Cepheid variable stars (see "Delta Cephei") within what was in 1923 called the Andromeda Nebula proved that what was thought to be a cloud of gas within the Milky Way is actually a distant and huge galaxy—and the study of galaxies beyond our own began. The Andromeda Galaxy was observed as long ago as the 10th century, although people then had no idea what it was. With a small telescope, notice its very small nucleus; notice too that the northwest region has a sharper edge than does the southeast; this edge is caused by dark dust lanes visible with a large telescope. Very large amateur telescopes show several dust lanes, enormous clouds of hydrogen gas, and even the largest globular clusters.

M32 and **NGC 205:** The Andromeda Galaxy's two brightest satellite galaxies are much smaller and fainter than M31, but they are easy to locate because they are so near to it. They can be seen in good binoculars on a dark night. Both are elliptical galaxies with magnitudes of 8 and 8.5, respectively. M32 is the second-best galaxy in the northern sky to see through a telescope, and it would be one of the showpieces of the sky were it not so completely overshadowed by its neighbor, M31. It is compact, with a diameter of less than 10,000 light years. NGC 205 has a lower surface brightness and is more elliptical, with a nearly 3:1 ratio (long:short dimension). NGC 205 is often called M110, although Messier never included it in his catalog.

Open Star Cluster NGC 752: Large and easy to locate, this cluster of at least 60 stars is 1½ degrees (actually, 20 light years) in diameter and magnitude 5.5. It lies a little more than a thousand light years from Earth.

AQUARIUS—the Water Carrier (a-**kware**-ee-us)
(chart 6)

"Helix Nebula" NGC 7293: The Helix has the largest apparent size of any planetary nebula, and through a large telescope it looks like a huge but very faint smoke ring half the size of our moon. Despite its relative brightness at magnitude 7, it is so diffuse that using very low power under the darkest of skies is necessary to see it at all. It appears large because it is so close; at 300 light years it is probably the nearest planetary. Its true diameter is about 1 light year. Large telescopes show it as an oval ring (ratio 5:4) with a darker center.

"Saturn Nebula" NGC 7009: Its vague resemblance to the planet Saturn gives this bright 8th-magnitude oval nebula its name. With a diameter of 25 arcseconds, it is easy to spot in a telescope, although no bright stars are present to guide your way to it. It is about 3,000 light years distant and about a light year in diameter (the same true size as the Helix Nebula, which is 10 times closer). Its central star is magnitude 11.5.

Globular Star Cluster M2: Located in a lonely part of the sky, this magnitude-6.5 cluster of stars is 37,000 light years distant. A giant among globulars, it is 150 light years in diameter and more than 300,000 times as luminous as our sun. It is highly concentrated, noticeably elliptical, and almost ¼ degree in diameter.

ARIES—the Ram (**air**-eez)
(chart 2)

Double Star Gamma Arietis: The faintest and southernmost of three bright stars that form Aries, this is one of the first double stars discovered (by Robert Hooke in 1664). It constitutes a pair of equally bright, white 4.8-magnitude stars, each 70 times the luminosity of our sun, which lie 7 arcseconds apart. At a distance of 120 light years, their true separation is at least 25 billion miles (250 times the distance from the earth to the sun).

AURIGA—the Charioteer (aw-**ree**-ga)
(chart 3)

Several bright 6th-magnitude open star clusters bunch together in the middle of Auriga. They are only a few degrees apart, and more than one are visible at the same time in binoculars. Fainter ones lie nearby.

Open Star Cluster M36: With an angular diameter of ⅙ degree, M36 is the smallest of Auriga's bright star clusters. Its true diameter is only 14 light years. At 4,000 light years from Earth, its brightest stars are 9th magnitude.

Open Star Cluster M37: Perhaps 200 light years more distant than M36 and twice the actual diameter, M37 has twice as many stars—though they are a full 2 magnitudes fainter. Its apparent diameter is ¼ degree.

Open Star Cluster M38: The same apparent as well as true size as M37, M38 is twice as faint but has brighter stars (though not as bright as those in M36). The appearances of M36, M37, and M38, all of which lie roughly the same distance from Earth, reflect their ages: M36, the youngest (perhaps 25 million years), has very bright but short-lived blue giants; M38 is twice as old and its brighter stars are yet comparatively fainter; M37, several times older still, has lost all its brightest stars.

Open Star Cluster NGC 1664: This cluster, some 3,700 light years distant, is magnitude 7.5.

Open Star Cluster NGC 1893: Large and distant, 7.5-magnitude NGC 1893 fills a circle almost ½ degree in diameter. It lies a whopping 13,000 light years from Earth. Its true diameter is 40 light years—enormous for an open star cluster.

Open Star Cluster NGC 2281: Bright, compact, and nearby, this 5.5-magnitude cluster of at least 30 stars is a relatively close 1,500 light years distant. It is 7 light years across.

BOÖTES—the Herdsman (bo-oh-teez)

(charts 4 and 5)

Double Star Epsilon Bootis: The brighter 2.7-magnitude yellow star is a scant 3 arcseconds from its blue 5th-magnitude companion. Nicknamed "Pulcherrima" ("the most beautiful") by its discoverer, this is one of the lovelier double stars in the sky, although steady air and a good telescope are needed to split them. The stars, which are 200 light years from Earth, are separated by at least 150 times the distance from the earth to the sun. They orbit too slowly for their motion to be measured.

Triple Star Mu Bootis: Initially this wide object appears to be two stars of magnitudes 4.3 and 6.5, separated by 108 arcseconds; it can be split in steadily held binoculars. Closer inspection shows that the fainter member is actually two sunlike stars of magnitudes 6.5 and 7.2, separated by 2 arcseconds. The stars are 120 light years distant and are separated by at least 4,000 times the distance from the earth to the sun (or at least 100 times the distance of Pluto from the sun).

Double Star Pi Bootis: These stars of magnitudes 4.9 and 5.8 are separated by 6 arcseconds. They are over 100 light years from Earth.

Double Star Xi Bootis: This pair, which lies 8 degrees east of Arcturus, was discovered in 1780 by William Herschel. Only 22 light years away, it constitutes a yellow solar type star of magnitude 4.7 and a yellow-orange star of magnitude 7.0, separated by 6 arcseconds. The actual separation is the same as Pluto's distance from the sun.

Globular Star Cluster NGC 5466: Look for this 9th-magnitude cluster (the faintest globular listed in this book) 10 degrees north of Arcturus. It is 54,000 light years distant and 55,000 times as luminous as our sun. The much brighter globular M3 lies 5 degrees directly west.

CAMELOPARDALIS—the Giraffe (ka-mel-o-par-da-liss)
(chart 1)

Open Star Cluster NGC 1502: This 6th-magnitude cluster of at least 45 stars is ¼ degree in diameter. At a distance of 2,600 light years, its actual diameter is only 7 light years. Its brightest stars are 7th magnitude.

Spiral Galaxy NGC 2403: This galaxy is part of the Ursa Major Group, which includes M81 and M82 some 14 degrees distant. It is not easy to find in a part of the sky void of bright stars to guide the way. This large 8.5-magnitude spiral with a tiny core lies about 8 million light years distant.

CANCER—the Crab (can-sir)
(chart 3)

Double Star Iota Cancri: This wide pair resembles the more famous Beta Cygni. A yellowish orange star at magnitude 4.0 is separated by 30 arcseconds from its magnitude-6.6 bluish neighbor. They are several hundred light years from Earth.

"Beehive" Open Star Cluster M44: Although Cancer has no bright stars, it does have one of the brightest and most attractive open star clusters. Today known as the Beehive, in classical times it was called Praesepe (Latin for "manger"). Smack in the middle of Cancer, the 3rd-magnitude Beehive is visible without binoculars on the darkest of nights, when it looks like a fuzzy little patch of light just over a degree in diameter. Good binoculars or a small telescope will show several dozen faint stars; the cluster has at least 50. The Beehive is 580 light years away and about 12 light years in diameter.

Open Star Cluster M67: Almost 10 degrees to the south of the Beehive, M67 is 1/30 as bright and ½ degree in diameter. It lies about 2,500 light years away (1,500 light years farther than the Beehive) and its brightest stars are 9th magnitude. It contains 200 known stars and certainly as many more whose membership remains unconfirmed. One of the oldest open star clusters known, it is at least several billion years old. Few open star clusters retain their identity for so long, and most disperse relatively quickly.

CANES VENATICI—the Hunting Dogs (kay-nis vay-nat-i-see)
(chart 4)

Double Star Cor Caroli: Also known as Alpha Canum Venaticorum, these two white stars (some observers report hints of color) are separated by 19 arcseconds. The stars, magnitudes 2.9 and 5.6, lie 110 light years from Earth. They are separated by at least 60 billion miles (15 times the distance of Pluto from the sun).

Globular Cluster M3: This bright 6th-magnitude globular contains half a million stars and is 300,000 times as luminous as our sun. It lies 33,000 light years distant. Look for it halfway between Arcturus and Cor Caroli.

"Whirlpool Galaxy" M51: The first galaxy whose spiral shape was recognized (by Ireland's Lord Rosse in 1845), this face-on spiral with its irregular companion is visible in any amateur telescope (and even good binoculars), and it remains the galaxy whose spiral structure is easiest to observe. Look for it 3½ degrees southwest of Alkaid, the end star in the handle of the Big Dipper. M51's high surface brightness makes it easier to see than its magnitude (8.5) would suggest. It is accompanied by a 9.5-magnitude irregular galaxy 4 arcminutes to the north, known as NGC 5195; an extension of a spiral arm links them. The companion is apparently a galaxy experiencing a "hit-and-run" collision with M51. Both are about 37 million light years from Earth. M51 was discovered by Charles Messier in 1773 as he was observing a comet pass nearby (its companion was discovered 8 years later).

Spiral Galaxy M63: This large 8.5-magnitude spiral (10 × 6 arcminutes in apparent size) is about the same dimensions as our Milky Way. It has a small starlike nucleus. Nicknamed the Sunflower for its patchy, sparse spiral arms, it is about 37 million light years distant.

Spiral Galaxy M94: A huge face-on spiral, this 8th-magnitude giant is 7 × 3 arcminutes in size, with a very bright nucleus surrounded by tightly wound spiral arms. It is 33 million light years away.

Spiral Galaxy M106: This large and bright 8.5-magnitude spiral has a similar orientation to M31. It is distinctly elongated in a 2:1, ratio with spiral arms that are visible in large amateur telescopes. It is about 25 million light years distant.

CANIS MAJOR—the Large Dog (kay-nis may-jor)
(chart 7)

Open Star Cluster M41: So bright that it can easily be seen without binoculars on dark winter evenings, 4 degrees south of Sirius, this 4th magnitude group of at least 80 stars is 2,000 light years distant and 25 light years in diameter. It is ⅔ degree in apparent size and its brightest stars are 7th magnitude. M41 is about 200 million years old—somewhat old for an open cluster.

Open Star Cluster NGC 2362: The other 4th-magnitude star cluster in Canis Major lies farther south, near the dog's tail. It is more than twice as distant, half the true diameter, and an eighth the apparent diameter of its more famous neighbor, M41.

CAPRICORNUS—the Sea Goat (cap-re-korn-us)
(charts 6 and 9)

Globular Star Cluster M30: This 7th-magnitude cluster of stars is ⅓ degree in diameter (about 80 light years in reality). It lies 25,000 light years from Earth in the northern part of Capricornus. It is 75,000 times as luminous as our sun.

CASSIOPEIA—Queen Cassiopeia (kass-ee-oh-pee-ya)
(charts 1 and 2)

Double Star Eta Cassiopeiae: These nearby stars, only 19 light years distant, are a magnitude 3.5 yellow star similar to our sun and a magnitude 7.5 reddish star separated from it by 11 arcseconds. They are noted for their striking color contrast. The actual separation between them is 6 billion miles (1½ times the distance from the sun to Pluto), and they take about 500 years to complete one orbit.

Triple Star Iota Cassiopeiae: One of the loveliest triple stars in the sky (and one that is visible most of the year), this trio comprises a white primary star of magnitude 4.5 with a 7.6-magnitude companion 2½ arcseconds distant. A third star of magnitude 8.6 lies 5 arcseconds from the brightest star (and 7 arcseconds from that star's close companion). The very neighborly pair need over 800 years to complete one orbit and the third star even longer. The trio lies 140 light years from Earth. Its brightest star is 30 times the luminosity of the sun.

Open Star Cluster M52: This rich cluster is 7th magnitude and relatively easy to spot. Its brightest stars are 8th-magnitude giants. It has a distance of 5,100 light years and a true diameter of about 20 light years (its apparent diameter is ¼ degree). With 100 known member stars, it is a relatively youthful 35 million years old.

Open Star Cluster M103: Half as bright and a third the size of M52, M103 has fewer stars, most of which are 9th magnitude and visible in any telescope, although not in binoculars. It is 8,000 light years distant.

Open Star Cluster NGC 457: This distant cluster is more than 11,000 light years from Earth. It is truly huge, with a diameter of 35 light years (⅓ degree in our sky), the brightest of which are 8th-magnitude young giants only about 10 million years old.

Open Star Cluster NGC 663: The same age and true size as NGC 457, NGC 663 likewise has 8th-magnitude young giants as its brightest stars. The cluster itself is 7th magnitude, and it is 7,200 light years from Earth and ¼ degree in apparent diameter.

Open Star Cluster NGC 7789: This 7th-magnitude star cluster of at least 300 known member stars (more than any other cluster in this book) is 6,000 light years from Earth and 30 light years in diameter. Its brighter stars are 10th magnitude.

CEPHEUS—King Cepheus (sef-ee-us or see-fus)
(chart 1)

Double Star Beta Cephei: These two giant stars are 4,000 times and 50 times, respectively, as luminous as our sun and perhaps 1,000 light years from Earth. Their actual separation is at least 400 billion miles (over 100 times the distance from Pluto to the sun), and they take thousands of years to complete one orbit. The primary star is a magnitude-3.2 blue-white star. Its white 8th-magnitude companion (¹⁄₁₀₀ as bright) is 13 arcseconds distant.

Variable/Double Star Delta Cephei: Astronomers find the distances to faint galaxies by observing certain variable stars—stars that change their brightnesses in regular and predictable ways. We know the true, intrinsic brightness of such stars so that when we identify one in a distant galaxy, we can compute how far away it must be to appear as bright as it does. The brightest of these Cepheid variable stars and the group's prototype is 4th-magnitude Delta Cephei. Watch it carefully (compare it to nearby 4.2-magnitude Epsilon and 3.4-magnitude Zeta), and you will see that it grows brighter and then fainter by a factor of 2 from magnitude 3.6 to 4.3, during a cycle that lasts 5 days, 8 hours, and 48 minutes. During this cycle, the unstable supergiant, which is 3,000 times as luminous as our sun and about 25 million miles in diameter, swells and shrinks by about 6 percent. Although faint to the naked eye, this is one of the most famous stars in the sky. A double star, Delta is also very lovely in a small telescope. Its 6.3-magnitude blue-white companion is 41 arcseconds from the supergiant; their actual separation is at least 1 trillion miles, or ⅕ light year.

CETUS—the Whale (see-tus)
(charts 2 and 6)

Mira, The "Wonderful Star": Although Cetus has no *bright* stars, it does have one very *interesting* star. Mira, also known as Omicron Ceti, is a pulsating red giant, which changes its brightness by more than 100 times in a cycle that lasts approximately 11 months. Eight of those months it is 9th magnitude and too faint to see without a telescope, but at its brightest it reaches 3rd or 4th magnitude—or occasionally brighter—and becomes one of the brightest stars of Cetus. This represents a change in luminosity of several hundred times. At its brightest, Mira is a true giant, some 400 times the diameter of our sun and large enough to fill our solar system to the orbit of Mars; at its smallest it is about the size of our sun. It lies about 220 light years distant. The star's variability was first noted in 1596, and it was named Mira ("wonderful" in Latin) by Johannes Hevelius in 1662.

Planetary Nebula NGC 246: Although rated at 8th-magnitude, this nebula seems fainter. Large for a planetary nebula, it boasts a diameter of 4 arcminutes. It lies about 1,300 light years from Earth. Its central star is magnitude 12.

Spiral Galaxy M77: The brightest member of a small group of galaxies, M77 is a magnificent spiral considerably larger than the Milky Way. Its broad spiral arms appear in larger telescopes; in smaller instruments, its small center stands out. Not visible with amateur equipment is a region of intense star formation and its quasarlike core, which generates radio waves. This magnitude-9.5 galaxy lies about 60 million light years from Earth.

COMA BERENICES—Berenice's Hair (ko-ma bear-ah-ni-sez)
(chart 4)

Coma Star Cluster: The swarm of faint stars which constitutes the constellation Coma Berenices lies midway between Boötes and Leo; and in ancient Greek times it was considered a part of Leo. It appears high in the sky all spring and overhead during the early evening in May. The stars of the constellation are actually a star cluster—a group of dozens of stars traveling together through space. Called the Coma Star Cluster, this group is about 290 light years away and 400 million years old. It is so large (5 degrees in diameter—about the size of the bowl of the Big Dipper) that it is best seen with the naked eye on a very dark night or with binoculars; a telescope shows only part of it at a time. The brighter stars are 5th and 6th magnitudes. The only closer bright cluster of stars, the Hyades in Taurus, is half as distant.

Double Star 24 Comae Berenices: These two stars, one yellow and the other blue white, with magnitudes 5.0 and 6.6, respectively, are 20 arcseconds apart. Forming a beautiful pair, they lie several hundred light years from Earth.

Globular Star Cluster M53: Fifteen degrees straight west of Arcturus is this 7.5-magnitude cluster. Larger and more distant than most, it is more than 200 light years in diameter and 60,000 light years distant. It is 270,000 times more luminous than our sun.

Spiral Galaxy M64: Nicknamed the Black-Eye Galaxy for the ring of dark dust surrounding its bright core, this 8.5-magnitude spiral galaxy lies in the direction of the Virgo Cluster of Galaxies. However, it is a foreground object half as far away as that cluster.

CORONA BOREALIS—(kor-oh-na bore-ee-al-is)
(chart 5)

Double Star Sigma Coronae Borealis: The 5.6-magnitude white primary star has an orange 6.6-magnitude companion 8 arcseconds distant. At a distance of 70 light years, their actual separation is roughly 200 times the distance from the earth to the sun, and they require about a thousand years to complete a single orbit.

Double Star Zeta Coronae Borealis: These about equally bright giant bluish stars are separated by 6½ arcseconds. They are magnitudes 5.1 and 6.0 and are roughly 500 light years from Earth. Their orbital motion is too slow to measure.

CORVUS—the Crow (kor-vis)
(chart 8)

Double Star Delta Corvi: Also known as Algorab, this beautiful pair was discovered by John Herschel in 1823. They are magnitudes 3.0 and 8.5 and are separated by 24 arcseconds. At a distance of 90 light years, their actual separation is 60 billion miles—15 times the distance from Pluto to the sun.

CYGNUS—the Swan (sig-nus)
(charts 2 and 5)

Double Star Beta Cygni: Also called Albireo (al-**beer**-e-oh), this is perhaps the loveliest double star of all, a showpiece at summer star parties. One star is blue and the other is yellow, creating a color contrast that is striking even in a small telescope. The yellow star is magnitude 3.1 and a giant, 700 times the luminosity of our sun; the blue star, at magnitude 5.1, is 120 times as luminous as our sun. The two stars lie a comfortable 34 arcseconds apart. At a distance of 400 light years, they are separated by at least 400 billion miles, or 100 times the distance from Pluto to the sun.

Double Star 61 Cygni: This is one of the nearest of all double stars, at a distance of only 11 light years (the same distance as Procyon and not much farther than Sirius). The pair, magnitudes 5.2 and 6.0, appear faint because they are dwarf stars, each about half the diameter and ¹⁄₂₀ the luminosity of our own sun. Both are orange, and they are separated by 30 arcseconds, which in reality is 10 billion miles—more than twice the distance of Pluto from the sun.

"North America Nebula" NGC 7000: Three degrees east of Deneb is a luminous cloud called the North America Nebula because of its distinctive shape, especially apparent in photographs. It is visible in good binoculars on a truly dark night, though a low-power wide-angle telescope is the best instrument with which to view it. Its apparent dimensions are 1½ × 2 degrees, while its true dimensions are about 60 × 50 light years, at a distance of 1,600 light years (the same as the Orion Nebula).

Planetary Nebula NGC 6826: This 9th-magnitude pale blue disk has an 11th magnitude central star. It is 25 arcseconds across and about 3,000 light years distant.

Open Star Cluster M29: This 6½-magnitude cluster is easy to find near the center of the cross of Cygnus. Its apparent diameter of only ⅙ degree equals 8 light years at its distance of 4,300 light years. Its brighter stars are 9th magnitude blue giants. One of the younger star clusters, it is a mere 10 million years old. It lies behind thin clouds of interstellar gas and dust, which dim it significantly.

Open Star Cluster M39: This nearby cluster of at least several dozen stars from magnitudes 7 to 10 is 900 light years distant. Its age is about 300 million years. It is large enough, with an apparent diameter of ½ degree, and bright enough, at magnitude 4.5, to see with the naked eye. View with binoculars or low-power wide-angle eyepieces.

Open Star Cluster NGC 6910: Lying ½ degree north of Gamma Cygni (Albireo), this 7.5-magnitude cluster is easily visible in binoculars. It is about ⅙ degree in diameter and almost 5,000 light years from Earth. It is only about 10 million years old, and its many bright stars would be a startling sight were it closer.

"Veil Nebula" NGC 6992-5, NGC 6960: The far-flung remains of a star that exploded more than 30,000 years ago, the Veil is a disconnected series of arcs of luminous gas with an overall diameter of 3 degrees. Through a large telescope on a very dark night, the brighter arcs look like strands of smoke. The brightest section is NGC 6960, a 1-degree-long strand running past 52 Cygni. Use low power.

DELPHINUS—the Dolphin (del-fi-nus)
(chart 5)

Double Star Gamma Delphini: These two yellow stars, each several times more luminous than our sun, are magnitudes 4.3 and 5.1 and are separated by 10 arcseconds. They are 100 light years distant, and their true separation is almost 10 times the distance of Pluto from the sun.

DRACO—the Dragon (dray-ko)
(charts 1 and 5)

Double Star Nu Draconis: The faintest of the four stars that form the trapezoid of Draco's head, these two equally bright 4.9-magnitude white stars are separated by

62 arcseconds—wide enough to each be visible in binoculars. Their actual separation is 2,000 times the distance from the earth to the sun (50 times the distance from Pluto to the sun), and they lie a distance of 100 light years from Earth.

Double Star Psi Draconis: This yellow star (magnitude 4.6) and orange star (magnitude 5.8) are separated widely enough (by 30 arcseconds) to be easily split in a small telescope. They are 70 light years from Earth, and their true separation is 700 times the distance from the earth to the sun.

Triple Star 16-17 Draconis: A wide 90 arcseconds separates two white stars of magnitudes 5.1 and 5.5. They are roughly 400 light years from Earth, and their true separation is at least ⅙ light year (more than 10,000 times the distance from the earth to the sun). The slightly fainter star (17 Draconis) forms a double with a 6.6-magnitude companion only 3 arcseconds distant.

Planetary Nebula NGC 6543: Its blue-green color gives this 8th-magnitude nebula its common name: the Cat's Eye Nebula. Use high power to see its small disk, only 18 arcseconds in diameter. It has an 11th magnitude central star. The nebula is about 3,600 light years distant.

ERIDANUS—the River (eh-rid-a-nus)
(charts 6 and 7)

Double Star 32 Eridani: Located to the right of Orion, these magnitude 4.7 and 6.1 stars are separated by 7 arcseconds. At an estimated distance of 300 light years, their true separation is several hundred times the distance from the earth to the sun.

Planetary Nebula NGC 1535: This 9th-magnitude pale green disk is 18 arcseconds in diameter, with a 12th-magnitude central star. Use high power.

GEMINI—the Twins (gem-eh-nye)
(chart 3)

Double Star Delta Geminorum: These dwarf stars, magnitudes 3.5 and 8.5, are separated by 6 arcseconds. At a distance of 59 light years, their true separation is 100 times the distance from the earth to the sun, and they take a thousand years to complete a single orbit.

Planetary Nebula NGC 2392: Despite its faintness at 10th magnitude, this object is well known. It is also one of the youngest known planetaries. Nicknamed the Eskimo Nebula (for its resemblance in photographs to a face surrounded by the hood of a parka), it is very small, with a diameter of only 13 arcseconds. It looks starlike in a small telescope or under low power; use high magnification to see its bluish disk. It is 3,000 light years distant and less than half a light year in diameter.

Open Star Cluster M35: Large (½ degree in diameter) and bright (5th magnitude), M35 is easily visible with the naked eye and is splendid in binoculars (less so in a telescope, which magnifies it too much). It lies about 2,700 light years distant. More than 20 light years in diameter, it contains 200 known member stars, the brightest of which are 8th magnitude. M35 is about 70 million years old—the same age as the smaller but closer Pleiades in nearby Taurus.

Open Star Cluster NGC 2129: Two degrees from M35 lies this more distant 6.5-magnitude cluster of 40 or more stars. It is also younger and, at a rather diminutive ⅒ degree, smaller. It is about 6,400 light years from Earth and about a dozen light years across.

HERCULES—the strong man Hercules (her-cue-leez)
(chart 5)

Double Star Alpha Herculis: This duo consists of an orange star (magnitude 3.5) and a bluish star (magnitude 5.4) separated by a mere 5 arcseconds. The brighter star is a true orange giant 400 times the diameter of the sun (large enough to fill the solar system to the orbit of Mars) and perhaps 1,000 times the luminosity of the sun. It and its companion lie several hundred light years from Earth and are separated by perhaps a thousand times the distance from the earth to the sun. Their orbital period is several thousand years.

Double Star Rho Herculis: This is another close pair, its stars of magnitude 4.5 and 5.5 separated by 4 arcseconds. They lie several hundred light years from Earth.

Double Star 95 Herculis: These two yellow-orange stars, equal in brightness with magnitudes 5.0 and 5.2, are separated by 6 arcseconds. Each star is about 100 times as luminous as the sun. The twosome is several hundred light years distant.

Planetary Nebula NGC 6210: This 9th-magnitude planetary is small (20 × 13 arc-seconds) but relatively bright. It looks starlike in a small telescope, so high magnification should be used to bring out its shape and blue color. It is 3,600 light years distant.

Globular Star Cluster M13: A showpiece of the sky, this bright cluster is a favorite at summer star parties. It is the most accessible star cluster from the Northern Hemisphere, its location to the north bringing it nearly overhead. Through small telescopes it looks like a fuzzy patch of light, but with a telescope at least 6 inches in diameter, the individual faint stars (the brightest are magnitude 12) begin to show. M13 is about 23,000 light years distant and, at magnitude 5.8, is barely visible to the naked eye though easy to see in binoculars. Look for it about a third of the way between the stars Eta and Zeta in the Keystone. It appears over ¼ degree in diameter (its true diameter is about 150 light years). M13 contains several hundred thousand stars and is 200,000 times as luminous as our sun. It was discovered by Edmond Halley, of Halley's Comet fame, in 1714.

Globular Star Cluster M92: Although relatively bright at magnitude 6.5, M92 is only half as bright as the more famous M13 only 10 degrees away and is therefore often overlooked. It lies only 3,000 light years farther from Earth than does M13, so the true sizes of these two clusters can be visually compared.

HYDRA—the female Water Snake (hi-dra)
(chart 8)

Open Star Cluster M48: Lying in a lonely part of the winter sky, this 5.5-magnitude cluster of several dozen 9th- to 13th-magnitude stars lies 1,500 light years from Earth. It is nearly 1 degree in diameter and easily visible in binoculars—once you know where to look.

Globular Star Cluster M68: This magnitude 7.75 cluster lies 33,000 light years from Earth. It is 70,000 times as luminous as our sun, and its stars are not very concentrated. Look for it less than 4 degrees south of the southeasternmost bright star in Corvus.

Planetary Nebula NGC 3242: Nicknamed the Ghost of Jupiter for its large size, this 8th-magnitude object lies in a desolate part of the sky. Its bright, light blue inner disk is about 40 arcseconds in diameter (the same apparent size as Jupiter). It is about 2,600 light years from Earth.

Spiral Galaxy M83: This bright 8th-magnitude supergiant lies face-on to Earth. It has hosted more supernovae (5) than any other galaxy except one. It is relatively nearby, at a distance estimated to be 15 million light years. M83 is nicknamed the Southern Pinwheel for its striking spiral structure featuring prominent dark dust lanes, seen through large telescopes.

LACERTA—the Lizard (la-ser-ta)
(charts 1, 2, and 5)

Open Star Cluster NGC 7209: Midway between Cygnus and Andromeda in the autumn sky is Lacerta the Lizard, whose deep space objects of note are two star clusters. NGC 7209 is almost 3,000 light years distant and about ¼ degree in diameter. Its brightest stars are 9th magnitude.

Open Star Cluster NGC 7243: This magnitude 6.5 cluster is 2,500 light years distant and is ½ degree in apparent diameter. Its brightest stars are visible in binoculars.

LEO—the Lion (lee-oh)
(chart 4)

Double Star Gamma Leonis: These two bright stars (magnitudes 2.6 and 3.8) complete an orbit every 6 centuries. They are 5 arcseconds apart, which, at a distance of 100 light years, translates to 150 times the distance from the earth to the sun. These are giant yellow stars, 90 and 30 times the luminosity of our sun.

Double Star 54 Leonis: Similar to Gamma Leonis but fainter and less colorful, these white stars are magnitudes 4.5 and 6.3. They are separated by 7 arcseconds.

Spiral Galaxies M65 and M66: Listed together because they lie only about ⅓ degree apart, south of the hindquarters of Leo, these two galaxies are visible in the same field of view using a low-power eyepiece. They are magnitudes 9½ and 9, respectively. Both are giant spirals of similar dimension and shape seen edge-on, with a ratio of almost 3:1. Both also have bright nuclei and dark dust lanes. A 10th magnitude edge-on spiral galaxy, NGC 3628, lies ½ degree north of the pair to complete what is called the Leo Triplet. The three are about 35 million light years distant.

Spiral Galaxy M96: This 9th-magnitude galaxy is the brightest of several that lie close together in central Leo. M95 is 0.5-magnitude fainter and ¾ degree to the west, while M105 is fainter still and 1 degree to the north. M96 is a tightly wound spiral, while M95 is a barred spiral and M105 a nearly round, bright elliptical. They are all about 40 million miles distant.

LEPUS—the Hare or Rabbit (leap-us)
(chart 7)

Double Star Gamma Leporis: This wide and relatively nearby pair is an easy target for small telescopes and even binoculars. Its solar-type stars are magnitudes 3.6 and 6.2 and are separated by 100 arcseconds. At a distance of 29 light years, their true separation is at least 900 times the distance from the earth to the sun, or 20 times the distance from Pluto to the sun. Their orbital period is too long to measure.

Globular Star Cluster M79: Twenty degrees west of Sirius lies this 7.5-magnitude moderately concentrated globular cluster. It is one of the few in the winter sky and a rarity during the colder months. It is 41,000 light years from Earth and more than 100,000 times as luminous as our sun. Rather small for its brightness, it has a diameter of 9 arcminutes (about 100 light years).

LYRA—the Harp (lie-ra)
(chart 5)

Triple Variable Star Beta Lyrae: These three stars form an interesting triangle. Their magnitudes are 3.5, 8, and 9; their separations, 46 and 67 arcseconds. They are about 150 light years distant and range from 140 to 3,000 times the sun's brilliance. The brightest star is itself actually two stars orbiting so close to each other that they are drawn into elliptical shapes and gas spirals from the larger to the smaller; as they orbit, the star varies from magnitude 3.4 to 4 in a cycle of 13 days.

Double-Double Star Epsilon Lyrae: With perfect eyesight (or binoculars), Epsilon Lyrae looks like two 5th magnitude stars of equal brightness separated by 209 arcseconds (about the minimum distance resolvable with the unaided eye). A telescope used with high power shows that each is actually a pair of stars very close to each other, making four in all. The angular separations of these two pairs are 2.3 and 2.5 arcseconds (their true separations are at least 15 billion miles). Each star is approximately 100 times the brightness of the sun, and their distance is about 180 light years.

"Ring Nebula" M57: A showpiece of the summer sky (partly because it is so easy to find), the Ring Nebula is the best-known planetary. Its shape is surprising. Through a good amateur telescope under high power it looks like a small and slightly elliptical 9th-magnitude smoke ring or Cheerio. Its true shape probably resembles an hourglass, but we see it from only one end. Its dimensions are 80 × 60 arcseconds and its density approximately 10,000 atomic particles per cubic centimeter (considered a vacuum on Earth). It is more than 1,000 light years distant and half a light year in diameter.

Globular Cluster M56: This 8.5-magnitude globular cluster is compact and difficult to resolve into stars. It is 7 arcminutes in diameter—half the size of M13 in nearby Hercules—and 32,000 light years distant.

MONOCEROS—the Unicorn (mo-no-ser-os)
(charts 3 and 7)

Triple Star Beta Monocerotis: This is one of the finest triple stars for small telescopes. The three white stars have roughly equal magnitudes (4.7, 5.1, and 6.1), and aligned they form a bent elbow with arms 7 and 3 arcseconds in length. These stars are about 150 light years from Earth. Use high magnification.

Open Star Cluster M50: This 6th-magnitude cluster of at least 80 known stars (the brightest of which are 8th magnitude) is 3,300 light years from Earth and about 15 light years in diameter. It has an apparent diameter of ¼ degree.

Open Star Cluster NGC 2353: 3½ degrees to the southeast of M50 lies this slightly larger but fainter 7th-magnitude cluster of perhaps a third as many stars. The two clusters are the same age (about 100 million years) and distance; they differ largely in their number of stars.

OPHIUCHUS—the Serpent Bearer (oh-fee-you-kus)
(charts 5 and 9)

Double Star 36 Ophiuchi: These two yellow-white stars, both magnitude 5.3, are separated by a mere 5 arcseconds. They lie 19 light years from Earth, and their true separation is at least as great as Pluto's from the sun.

Planetary Nebula NGC 6572: At first glance, this tiny 9th-magnitude nebula, only 8 arcseconds in diameter, looks starlike. High magnification brings out its bluish oval disk. It is about 2,000 light years distant.

Globular Star Cluster M9: Seven bright globular star clusters are located in Ophiuchus, plus many more for those who care to hunt them down. This 7.5-magnitude cluster is

27,000 light years distant and 130,000 times as luminous as our sun. About 70 light years in diameter, M9 is slightly elliptical.

Globular Star Cluster M10: The nearest and largest in apparent size (more than ¼ degree) of the globulars in Ophiuchus, 6.5-magnitude M10 is 80,000 times the luminosity of our sun. At 14,000 light years distant, its diameter is about 70 light years.

Globular Star Cluster M12: Almost a twin of slightly smaller M10, M12 is magnitude 6.7. It is 15,000 light years distant and 70,000 times the luminosity of the sun. Its diameter is about 75 light years.

Globular Star Cluster M14: At magnitude 7.25, M14 is over 300,000 times the luminosity of our sun. It lies 28,000 light years from Earth.

Globular Star Cluster M19: This huge 7th-magnitude cluster is 28,000 light years from Earth but only 5,000 light years from the core of the Milky Way. Tidal forces have distorted its shape into a noticeable ellipse about ¼ degree in diameter. It is an awesome 350,000 times as luminous as our sun.

Globular Star Cluster M62: A giant among giants, 6.25-magnitude M62 is almost 400,000 times as luminous as our sun. It lies 22,000 light years from Earth but only 6,000 light years from the center of the galaxy. Tidal forces have given it, like M19, an elliptical shape.

Globular Star Cluster M107: The faintest of the globulars listed here in Ophiuchus, this 8th-magnitude cluster is 21,000 light years away. Sixty light years in diameter, it is almost 60,000 times as luminous as our sun.

Open Star Cluster IC 4665: This 6th-magnitude open cluster is visible with binoculars, appearing as a patch of stars four times larger than the moon. It lies much closer than the globulars of Ophiuchus at a distance of 1,100 light years. IC 4665 has only a few dozen 7th- and 8-magnitude stars and is only abut 400 times as luminous as our sun. Its true diameter is 15 light years.

"Pipe Nebula": This dark nebula is similar to but smaller than the Great Rift in Cygnus. It extends for about 7 degrees south and southeast of Theta Ophiuchi, blocking light from the central hub of our galaxy. Some 5,000 or so light years from Earth, it has the shape of a tobacco pipe. Observe the Pipe Nebula with either the naked eye or binoculars on the darkest of moonless nights.

ORION—the Hunter (oh-rye-un)

(charts and 7)

Double Star Mintaka: This is the westernmost star of the three that form Orion's belt. It lies at the same distance as the Orion Nebula just below it—about 1,600 light years. With a magnitude of 2.2, this is a true giant, some 20,000 times the luminosity of our sun. Its 6.8-magnitude companion is 53 arcseconds away, which is about half a light year at such a distance, and the pair is one of the easiest double stars to locate with a small telescope.

Triple Star Iota Orionis: Located ½ degree south of the Orion Nebula and even more distant from Earth, this magnitude 2.9-star is another giant, with perhaps 20,000 times the luminosity of the sun. Its bluish 7.0-magnitude companion lies 11 arcseconds distant. A third star of 11th-magnitude lies 50 arcseconds away. A large scope shows hints of nebulosity in the area.

Multiple Star Sigma Orionis: This is another member of the Orion group of brilliant white stars. The main star is magnitude 3.7. A 6.7-magnitude companion lies 13 arcseconds distant, while a 9th-magnitude star lies 11 arcseconds farther away. A second companion is also 6.7-magnitude, though it lies a remote 42 arcseconds distant; in turn it has an 8th-magnitude companion 30 arcseconds away. This widespread group spans just over ⅓ light year.

Sextuplet Star Theta Orionis: This celebrated six-star system is embedded in the Orion Nebula, and anyone looking at the nebula sees at least its four brightest members. These four are blue-white giants with magnitudes 5.1, 6.7, 6.8, and 7.9, 400 to 5,000 times as luminous as the sun, and they form the famous "Trapezium." They are true giants. Two additional members of the system are two 11th-magnitude stars, one 4 arcseconds north of the westernmost star and the other 4 arcseconds southeast of the southernmost star of the Trapezium. All these stars were recently born from the gas of the Orion Nebula and may be no more than a few hundred thousand years old. They are indeed among the youngest stars of all.

Double Star Alnitak: This is the easternmost of the three stars of Orion's belt. The two white stars are magnitudes 1.9 and 4.0 and their separation is 2.4 arcseconds. They would be easier to observe as two distinct objects were they not so bright that they produce an obscuring glare. Use a good telescope and high magnification.

"Orion Nebula" M42 and M43: The jewel in Orion's sword is the brightest nebula in the sky. Four times the apparent size of the full moon, it is visible to the naked eye. We can only wonder how this glowing cloud of gas would fill our sky were it much closer than its actual distance of 1,600 light years. That it appears so bright from such a considerable distance attests to its true size and grandeur. Yet what we know as the Orion Nebula is only the bright central part of a cloud that fills much of the constellation of Orion and is 10 degrees in extent—the size of your open hand held at arm's length. It is lit by the four hot stars of the Trapezium, clustered tightly at the nebula's heart. These young stars were recently born, adding to the nebula's renown as a "stellar" nursery. The part we see is about 30 light years (a bit over 1 degree) across. With the naked eye, look for the Trapezium as a "fuzzy" star in Orion's sword. On dark nights, it is obvious in binoculars. In a large telescope, it is overwhelming. M42 constitutes the main mass, which fans away from the Trapezium at the center. M43 is a detached portion to the south, separated from M42 by a dark dust lane that lies in the foreground. M43 would be regarded as an immensely interesting object were it in any other part of the sky but next to M42, which overshadows it. M43 is lit by the 7th-magnitude variable star NU Orionis near its center. Study the great nebula under a variety of magnifications to see its unending delicate structure. Surprisingly, it was not discovered until 1610.

Reflection Nebula M78: Unlike the great Orion Nebula, which glows because of hot young stars within it, M78 merely reflects light from two faint 10th-magnitude stars embedded within it. It is the brightest "reflection nebula" in the sky (the more famous blue reflection nebula, which surrounds the Pleiades, is not visible with amateur equipment). Look for M78 2½ degrees above Alnitak using a good telescope. It is 6 × 8 arcminutes in extent. The same distance as the nearby Orion Nebula (1,600 light years), it is about 4 light years in diameter.

Bright Nebula NGC 2023: An 8th-magnitude star lies 0.4 degrees southeast of Alnitak; a small reflection nebula roughly 0.2 degrees in diameter surrounds this star and reflects its light. This nebula is a challenge to see!

Bright Nebula NGC 2024: Nicknamed the Flame Nebula, this splotch of luminous gas lies ¼ degree east of Alnitak. Large telescopes show a dark lane that splits it from north to south. Position your telescope so that glaring Alnitak stays outside the eyepiece's field of view. NGC 2024 is about ½ degree in diameter.

Bright Nebula NGC 2174: This large, nearly circular emission nebula near the feet of Gemini may be visible in large binoculars on an exceptionally dark night. Its dimensions are ⅔ degree × ½ degree, which at its distance of about 5,000 light years, translates to an actual diameter of about 35 light years. Its brightest part is a small central disk 1 arcminute across (about the apparent size of Jupiter). The nebula is lit by a very hot 7.5-magnitude blue star at its center.

PEGASUS—the Flying or Winged Horse (peg-a-sus)
(chart 2)

Globular Star Cluster M15: The densest globular cluster in the Milky Way, M15, at magnitude 6.25, is bright enough to see with binoculars. It is about 100 light years in diameter (⅓ degree as seen in the sky) and 33,000 light years distant. It is about 375,000 times as luminous as the sun.

PERSEUS—the hero Perseus (pur-see-us)
(charts 1, 2, and 3)

Algol, The Demon Variable Star: The name "Algol" derives from the medieval Arabic for "ghoul" or "demon." Observers centuries ago were alarmed to see this star grow noticeably fainter once every 3 days—something a good star was not supposed to do. It does seem to leisurely "wink" at us! Today we know that Algol (which is about 100 light years from Earth) is actually two stars in orbit around their common center of gravity. Their orbital plane is so aligned that, as seen from Earth, they eclipse each other once each orbit. (They are a binary star system, but too close together to see as separate stars.) When the brighter of the two stars is hidden by the fainter, Algol fades from magnitude 2.1 to 3.4 and becomes one-third as bright as normal for about 10 hours. Compare it with nearby Gamma Andromedae, which remains a constant magnitude 2.1, and Epsilon Persei at magnitude 2.9. Algol's variability may have been known in ancient Greek times. If so, it was rediscovered about 1667. *Sky & Telescope* magazine publishes the times of its monthly cycle, which lasts 2 days, 20 hours, and 49 minutes. The two stars that comprise Algol are each about 3 times the sun's diameter and are separated from each other by only their own diameter.

Planetary Nebula M76: Nicknamed the Little Dumbbell after its resemblance to the famous planetary in Vulpecula, this 10th magnitude nebula is easier to see than its magnitude would suggest. Relatively large, with dimensions of 2 × 1 arcminutes, it looks elongated even in a small telescope. Note its distinct green color, visible in large telescopes; M76 is one of the greenest bright objects in the sky.

"Perseus Double Cluster" NGC 869 and NGC 884: Halfway between the star Alpha Persei and the middle of the **W** of Cassiopeia is a pair of very distant 4.5-magnitude open star clusters. To the naked eye, they look like two faint stars so close together that our moon would just fit between them. They are especially lovely through binoculars or a small telescope, which shows hundreds of young stars in each cluster; the brightest of these stars are 6th and 7th magnitude. Only a few million years old, NGC 869 and NGC 884 contain supergiants that are nearly 100,000 times as luminous as our sun; they would rival Betelgeuse and Rigel were they closer. These are among the largest star clusters in our Milky Way, with true diameters of about 60 light years. Approximately 7,200 light years from Earth, they are in the Perseus Arm of the Milky Way—the spiral limb beyond the Orion Arm. Use binoculars or a very low power wide-angle telescope.

Open Star Cluster M34: This ample 5.5-magnitude cluster, the size of the full moon, is visible without a telescope along a line from Algol to Gamma Andromedae. At 1,400 light years distant, and 15 light years in diameter, its brightest stars are 8th magnitude. (One bright foreground star, magnitude 7.3, is not a member of the cluster.) It is about 190 million years old.

Open Star Cluster NGC 1342: At magnitude 6.5, this sparse, aged cluster is easy to spot with binoculars. It contains 40 known stars and certainly many more spread over ¼ degree of space. It is 1,700 light years distant and only 7 light years in diameter.

Open Star Cluster NGC 1528: Similar in size to M34 but a magnitude fainter, this cluster is 2,400 light years from Earth and almost 20 light years in diameter. It is quite attractive in binoculars.

Open Star Cluster NGC 957: Somewhat closer to Earth than the Double Cluster is, this 7.5-magnitude sparse cluster is about 6,500 light years distant and 20 light years across. It is older than the Double Cluster and has lost its brightest stars; those that remain are 9th magnitude and fainter.

PISCES—the Fishes (pie-sees)
(charts 2 and 6)

Double Star Psi¹ Piscium: This duo is separated by a comfortable 30 arcseconds. Magnitudes 5.2 and 5.6, they are roughly 400 light years from Earth.

Double Star Zeta Piscium: These two white stars, magnitudes 5.2 and 6.3, are separated by 23 arcseconds. They lie more than 100 light years from Earth.

Spiral Galaxy M74: This giant face-on spiral galaxy lies 15 degrees directly south of M33, in the eastern part of Pisces. With its primary two arms loosely wound, it has a very low surface brightness. It is magnitude 9.5 and about the same size as our Milky Way. It lies about 30 million light years from Earth.

PUPPIS—the Ship's Stern (pup-is)
(chart 7)

Open Star Cluster M46: Located in a richly populated part of the winter Milky Way to the east of Sirius, this cluster has a total magnitude of 6 although it contains more than a hundred stars between magnitudes 10 and 13. It is 5,300 light years distant and 35 light years in diameter. Its apparent diameter is ⅓ degree. A curious feature is a 10th-magnitude planetary nebula, NGC 2438, appearing near its center though in fact located between us and the cluster. This cluster is several hundred million years old.

Open Star Cluster M47: M47 lies 1½ degrees west of M46 and is visible along with it in binoculars. The two clusters, however, have very different appearances, since the brightest stars in M47 are only 6th magnitude. The cluster itself has a total magnitude of 5. It is 1,500 light years distant, 13 light years in true diameter, and ½ degree in apparent diameter. M47 is only 30 million years old yet retains relatively bright stars. It too has a curiosity near its center—a double star consisting of two 8th-magnitude stars separated by 7 arcseconds.

Open Star Cluster M93: At a distance of 3,500 light years, M93 has an apparent diameter of only ⅙ degree and a true diameter of 25 light years. Its 80 identified members appear 8th magnitude and fainter.

Open Star Cluster NGC 2423: Lying a mere ½ degree north of M47, this 7th-magnitude cluster is ⅕ degree in diameter and 2,400 light years distant.

Open Star Cluster NGC 2477: This 6th-magnitude cluster, ⅓ degree in apparent diameter, contains hundreds of stars 11th magnitude and fainter. An old cluster roughly 700 million years in age, it has lost its bright giants. It is 3,700 light years from Earth and 35 light years in diameter.

SAGITTA—the Arrow (sa-geet-a)
(chart 5)

Globular Star Cluster M71: This small and nearby 8th-magnitude globular is easy to find near the middle of its diminutive constellation. It is a mere 12,000 light years away. With a diameter of 25 light years (⅛ degree), it is only about 13,000 times as luminous as our sun. Its brightest stars are 12th magnitude. Very diffuse for a globular cluster, M71 resembles a compact open star cluster.

SAGITTARIUS—the Archer (sa-je-tare-ee-us)
(chart 9)

"Great Sagittarius Star Cloud," The Center of the Milky Way: The Milky Way's true center lies far beyond the nearby stars of Sagittarius. It is located 5 degrees to the west and slightly above the tip of the spout of the "teapot" outlined by the stars of Sagittarius and also above the tail of Scorpius. The center cannot be seen because intervening clouds of gas completely absorb light waves from it. Radio waves, however, pass through clouds, so the galaxy's center can be pinpointed and studied by radio astronomers. The Great Sagittarius Star Cloud is the visible part of the hub of the Milky Way. It pokes above clouds of obscuring gas and dust, appearing as an irregular cloud of distant stars several degrees in extent. It shows up well to the naked eye and looks even better in binoculars. About 30,000 light years away, it is as close to the center of the Milky Way as anything you will see in the sky.

"Small Sagittarius Star Cloud" M24: This enormous object, with dimensions of 1×2 degrees, is a roughly rectangular portion of the innermost arm of the Milky Way. It is visible through a window in the great clouds of gas that lie between us and the center of the galaxy. Like the Great Sagittarius Cloud, it pokes above the obscuring material that blocks the light of most of the galaxy's inner arm and central portion. The Small Cloud, which is half as far away as the Great Cloud, is conspicuous on a dark night once you know where to look, about 10 degrees north of the center of the constellation. Use binoculars or a low-power wide-angle telescope. (See Chapter 12, "Observing the Milky Way."

Open Star Cluster M18: This sparse cluster lies 1 degree south of the Omega Nebula. Only about ⅒ degree in diameter and 7th magnitude, it consists of two dozen 9th- to 11th-magnitude stars. It is nearly 4,000 light years away toward the center of the Milky Way and 10 light years in diameter. Its age is estimated at 30 million years.

Open Star Cluster M21: With 70 known stars of 8th magnitude and fainter, this cluster lies less than 1 degree northeast of the Trifid Nebula. It is the same distance as M18, and it too is 30 million years old. However, it is a magnitude brighter and several times the area (¼ degree in apparent diameter, 15 light years in reality). It is a more interesting sight through a telescope.

Open Star Cluster M23: This irregularly shaped 5.5-magnitude cluster has more than 150 stars 9th magnitude and fainter. It is ½ degree in diameter (the size of the full moon) and is a pretty sight in large binoculars and very low power telescopes. It has a distance of 2,000 light years and a diameter of about 17 light years.

Open Star Cluster M25: This bright (4½-magnitude) diffuse group of 30 stars is 5 degrees almost due north of the globular cluster M22 (contrast the stars in these two very different kinds of clusters). M25 is 2,300 light years distant, and its stars, scattered over an area equal in size to the full moon, are bright enough to be seen in binoculars. Its brightest star is a Cepheid variable (U Sagittarii) that ranges from magnitude 6.3 to 7.1 in a period of 6.74 days.

Globular Star Cluster M22: Sagittarius has far more than its fair share of bright globular clusters. The best known is M22, the first globular discovered (in 1665, if not earlier). Look for M22 less than 3 degrees to the upper left of the top of the "teapot" outlined by Sagittarius. Magnitude 5, it is visible to the naked eye on a dark night and is an easy object to see in binoculars. It is one of the closest globular clusters to Earth, with a distance of only 10,500 light years. It would be the most magnificent such cluster for observers in North America were it not so low in the sky. It appears gigantic, with a diameter of more than ⅓ degree (65 light years in reality), and its brightest stars are a bit brighter than 11th magnitude. This cluster is 200,000 times as luminous as our sun. Globular star clusters concentrate toward Sagittarius because they orbit the center of the Milky Way, and all pass through this part of the sky at one time or another before dispersing to the outer parts of their orbits, which lie in all directions across the sky.

Globular Star Cluster M28: Located a mere 1 degree from the top star of the "teapot," M28 is easy to locate. It is 7th magnitude and has 175,000 times the luminosity of our sun. It lies 19,000 light years from Earth.

Globular Star Cluster M54: Highly concentrated, this magnitude 7.5 cluster is a true giant, boasting 800,000 times the luminosity of our sun. It lies beyond the far side of our galaxy; at the great distance of 85,000 light years, it is one of the most distant objects visible in binoculars. It was recently discovered to be the nucleus of a tiny dwarf galaxy, called the Sagittarius Dwarf Elliptical Galaxy, the closest galaxy to our Milky Way. The cluster's apparent size of $\frac{1}{10}$ degree translates to a true diameter of 200 light years. Because of its great distance, it is resolvable into stars only in a very large telescope.

Globular Star Cluster M55: Lying some distance east of the other globulars of Sagittarius, M55 is more difficult to find. Nevertheless, its brightness (magnitude 6.25) and great size ($\frac{1}{3}$ degree) help you locate it. It is 17,000 light years distant, 85,000 times as luminous as the sun, and not very compact. Its brightest stars are 11th magnitude.

Globular Star Cluster M69: One of the fainter globulars in Messier's catalog (along with nearby M70), M69 is magnitude 7.5 and has a diameter of $\frac{1}{8}$ degree. At a distance of 27,000 light years, it has an actual diameter of about 55 light years. It is about 80,000 times as luminous as our sun.

Globular Star Cluster M70: A near twin of M69, M70 is slightly fainter (magnitude 8), more distant (28,000 light years), and less luminous (about 55,000 times the luminosity of our sun). Both are near the center of our galaxy.

"Lagoon Nebula" M8: This huge 5th-magnitude glowing cloud of gas and dust is roughly $1 \times \frac{1}{2}$ degree in size (twice the full moon) and barely visible to the naked eye. It is spectacular in a telescope, second only in splendor to the Great Nebula in Orion. A 2-arcminute-wide lane of dark dust (the "Lagoon") divides it. Much of the energy that causes the Lagoon to fluoresce comes from a hot young blue 7th-magnitude star, 9 Sagittarii; 9 Sagittarii is one of the hottest and brightest stars known, with a luminosity 1,600,000 times greater than the sun. The Lagoon's brightest part, 30 arcseconds across, is called the Hourglass Nebula; it is made to fluoresce by a hot young 9.5-magnitude star immediately to the west that may be no more than 10,000 years old. Stars are forming within the Hourglass at the present time. The open cluster NGC 6530 in the Lagoon's eastern part contains as many as 100 stars that formed as recently as 2 million years ago and that lie in front of the nebulosity beyond. Interestingly, the cluster was discovered before the nebula—a comment on the quality of small 17th-century refracting telescopes. At a distance of about 5,000 light years, the Lagoon is roughly 100×50 light years in extent.

"Omega Nebula" M17: Called the Omega, Swan, or Horseshoe, this nebula is smaller and more concentrated than M8 and its center has a higher surface brightness. Visible even in binoculars in the northern part of Sagittarius, it appears in a telescope as a curved arc, which is said to resemble the neck of a swan, a horseshoe, or the Greek letter

Ω (Omega). Dark clouds of material block the outer parts of the nebula to the north and west, giving it a relatively sharp edge in those directions, while to the south and east it fades off gradually. The hot stars that cause it to fluoresce are buried within it and therefore invisible to the star gazer. At a distance of about 6,000 light years, its apparent size is over ½ degree and its true extent about 40 light years. It is not far from M16 in Serpens.

"Trifid Nebula" M20: Although smaller and fainter than the nearby Lagoon, the Trifid is easier to see in a small telescope because of its greater compactness and higher surface brightness. The 8th-magnitude Trifid is just 1½ degrees north of M8, and the two fit comfortably within the same field of view in high-power binoculars. The name "Trifid" comes from the nebula's three-part structure, caused by three dust lanes that front and appear to trisect it. The Trifid, which appears to lie about 1,500 light years beyond the Lagoon, may not be associated with it. This nebula is ¼ degree in diameter, which translates to 30 light years in extent at a distance of 6,500 light years. The cluster of young stars within it was recently born from its gas. At its center is a triplet of stars of magnitudes 7.6, 8.7, and 10.7, reminiscent of the more luminous Trapezium at the heart of the Orion Nebula. The brightest of these stars provides the energy to ionize the nebula and cause it to fluoresce. A blue reflection nebula lies to the north around a 7.5-magnitude star, which is not hot enough to ionize the gas but close enough for its light to reflect off it. (This and M78 in Orion are the most interesting two reflection nebulae visible to amateurs.)

SCORPIUS—the Scorpion (skor-pee-us)
(chart 9)

Double Star Beta Scorpii: The bright northernmost star of the Scorpion's claws is one of the best double stars to view with a small telescope. With a separation of 14 arcseconds, it closely resembles famous Mizar in the Big Dipper. The white giant stars, magnitudes 2.6 and 4.9, are some 600 light years from Earth.

Quadruple Star Nu Scorpii: This double-double star is similar to famous Epsilon Lyrae but more challenging to see, especially in small telescopes. It consists of two primary pairs separated by a wide 41 arcseconds; these pairs are visible in any telescope as two stars of magnitudes 4.4 and 6.3. Close inspection shows the northernmost and fainter "star" to be in fact two stars of magnitudes 6.8 and 7.5, separated by only 2.3 arcseconds. The brighter "star" is two stars of magnitudes 4.4 and 6.9, separated by a mere 1.3 arcseconds. Nu Scorpii is 550 light years from Earth and the primary pairs are separated by ⅒ light year.

Open Star Clusters M6 and M7: Two especially large open star clusters, M6 and M7 (magnitudes 4.0 and 3.3), are easily visible to the naked eye. They were known (although their nature was not) in ancient times. They lie 4 degrees apart above the Scorpion's stinger. M6 is 2,400 and M7 is 800 light years distant, and their apparent diameters are ¼ degree and 1¼ degrees, respectively. In binoculars you can see them both together. Collectively, their brightest stars are 6th and 7th magnitude. Use binoculars on M7; even a low-power wide-angle telescope will not show it all at once. The astronomer Ptolemy in 130 A.D. called M7 a nebula.

Open Star Cluster NGC 6231: This interesting cluster of stars in the tail of the Scorpion, listed at 3rd magnitude, is easily visible to the naked eye. It is a cluster of about 40 very young hot giants and supergiants as bright as 5th magnitude and no older than 10 million years. These are among the most luminous stars known; they shine with up to 250,000 times the brilliance of our sun. The cluster is 6,000 light years distant and 30 light years in diameter (¼ degree as seen in the sky).

Open Star Cluster NGC 6383: A mere 1 degree west of M6 lies this small (¼ degree diameter) 5.5-magnitude group of 40 8th- and 9th-magnitude stars. It is easy to spot with M6 to guide the way. NGC 6383 is just over 4,000 light years distant and a youthful 10 million years old.

Globular Star Cluster M4: Lying 1⅓ degrees due west of Antares, this cluster, while huge (½ degree diameter—almost as big as the full moon!) and bright (magnitude 5.5), is barely visible to the naked eye. It seems to be the closest globular cluster of all with a distance of only 7,000 light years. Its brightest stars are 11th magnitude and visible in most amateur telescopes. It is 55 light years across and 60,000 times as luminous as our sun.

Globular Star Cluster M80: Lying midway between Antares and Beta Scorpii, M80 is easy to find. It is magnitude 7.25, 28,000 light years distant, and 125,000 times as luminous as our sun. It is ⅙ degree in diameter.

SCUTUM—the Shield (skyoo-tum)
(chart 9)

Scutum lies just south of the Great Rift that splits the Milky Way. Two large "star clouds" (dense portions of the Milky Way), bright enough to see with the unaided eye, make the area a very enjoyable place to explore with binoculars and wide-angle telescopes.

Open Star Cluster M11: This showpiece of the summer sky is many observers' favorite star cluster. Although not as bright as many others (it is 6th magnitude), it is compact and has dozens of nicely spaced and equally bright stars 10th magnitude and fainter, making it a very pleasing sight in telescopes of all sizes. Look for M11 near the bottom of a small ring of naked-eye stars. While most open star clusters have up to a hundred stars, M11 contains nearly a thousand; it somewhat resembles a loose globular cluster. It is about 5,400 light years from Earth and 20 light years in diameter. Approximately 200 million years old, it has about 9,000 times the luminosity of our sun. It is nicknamed the Flying Duck Cluster for its resemblance to a flight of wild ducks.

Open Star Cluster M26: This 8th-magnitude cluster lies almost as distant as M11 and is the same true diameter. However, it is a poor second as seen through a telescope, because it has far fewer stars and is not nearly as compact. Its 30 or so stars of 11th magnitude occupy an area of the sky about ⅙ degree in diameter.

Globular Star Cluster NGC 6712: This 8th-magnitude cluster is 22,000 light years from Earth, ⅛ degree in diameter, and 80,000 times as luminous as our sun.

SERPENS—the Serpent or snake (sir-pens)
(charts 5 and 9)

Double Star Theta Serpentis: This double star is beautiful in a small telescope. The two white stars are magnitudes 4.5 and 5.4, and they are separated by 22 arcseconds. At a distance of 100 light years, the actual distance between them is at least 100 billion miles. Their orbital motion is too slow to detect.

Globular Star Cluster M5: This magnificent globular cluster rivals M13 in Hercules. At magnitude 5.5, it can be seen with binoculars (and with the naked eye on the darkest of nights). Lying 24,000 light years from Earth, it appears to be ¼ degree in diameter (corresponding to a true diameter of 130 light years). Its brightest stars are 12th magnitude. The entire cluster is about 270,000 times as luminous as our sun. It is one of the oldest globular clusters known.

"Eagle Nebula" and Open Star Cluster M16: Some of the Hubble Space Telescope's most spectacular photographs show the towering columns and pillars of gas of the Eagle Nebula, where stars are even now being born from clouds of hydrogen. Although a backyard telescope will show far less, the 6½-magnitude Eagle Nebula remains an easy target on a dark night. Unfortunately, there are no bright stars nearby to guide the way. The cluster of 100 stars scattered around the nebula is physically related to it; the cluster's stars were recently born from it. The brightest stars (which are 8th magnitude) have 1 million times the sun's luminosity and are not very old. The designation "M16" properly refers to the star cluster, as that is what Messier noted with his small refracting telescope and therefore cataloged in 1764, though the two are inseparable. Nevertheless, the nebula is far more interesting. The entire complex is perhaps 9,000 light years distant, and the nebula's diameter is about 70 light years. The nebula's colorful pillars are visible in a large amateur instrument; they are up to a light year long; look for new stars forming at their tips. An alternative name, Star Queen Nebula, proposed by Robert Burnham in his *Celestial Handbook*, is gaining popularity.

TAURUS—the Bull (tore-us)
(chart 3)

Double Star 118 Tauri: Located midway between the tips of the Bull's horns, this double star is easy to find. Its components are magnitude 5.8 and 6.6 and are separated by 5 arcseconds. The pair is several hundred light years distant. Use medium and high magnifications.

"Hyades Star Cluster": The Bull's face is a cluster of bright stars called the Hyades (**hi**-a-deez), which is so close to Earth we can easily see the individual stars with unaided eyesight. It looks even better in binoculars. A telescope, however, restricts the field of view. The cluster has an apparent diameter of 5½ degrees, which corresponds to a true diameter of 15 light years—typical for open clusters. Actually, we notice only its core; outlying 6th magnitude stars lie up to 12 degrees (40 light years) from its center. Many of the Hyades stars are red and yellow, in contrast with the younger Pleiades, which has blue and white stars. The Hyades is the closest major cluster, with a distance of 151 light years from Earth. It is a somewhat old open cluster, with an estimated age of 700 million years. Aldebaran, which happens to lie in front of the stars of the Hyades, is not, however, part of the cluster.

"Pleiades Star Cluster" M45: The Pleiades (**plee**-ah-deez) is a beautiful cluster of stars that rises an hour before the main part of Taurus. At one time, the Pleiades was considered a separate constellation, but now it forms part of the Bull. Although called the Seven Sisters in Greek mythology (they are the seven daughters of the Titan Atlas), the cluster actually contains six bright (along with many faint) stars; this designation is therefore a source of endless speculation. It is possible, though highly unlikely, that one star has faded since ancient Greek times. In any case, you might see 10 or so stars if your eyesight is exceptionally good, and binoculars will show several dozen; the total is at least 200 and perhaps as high as 500. The Pleiades looks like a very little dipper about 1 degree wide. It is a relatively young cluster (roughly 100 million years old), with bright blue stars 380 light years from Earth and about 12 light years across. Long-exposure photographs show blue nebulosity surrounding the stars. This phenomenon represents a cloud of dust the stars happen to be passing through, which reflects the light of the blue stars near it; contrary to some reports, this is not dust out of which the cluster formed. That dust dispersed long ago. Use binoculars but not a telescope.

Open Star Cluster NGC 1647: Located between the horns of the Bull, this 6th-magnitude cluster is overshadowed by the Hyades, less than 4 degrees distant. It is about 1,700 light years from Earth—more than 10 times as far as the Hyades. Its 200 or more stars fill an area ⅔ degree in diameter.

Open Star Cluster NGC 1746: The same apparent size as NGC 1647 but with only a tenth as many stars, NGC 1746 would be a poorer sight were its stars not a magnitude brighter. It shines with a combined magnitude of 6 and it too lies within Taurus's horns. It is about 1,300 light years distant.

"Crab Nebula" M1: This "supernova remnant" is the remains of a star that exploded almost a thousand years ago, in 1054 A.D. It consists of a small 9th-magnitude nebula with a *pulsar*—a rapidly rotating neutron star that emits pulses of radio energy—at its core. The pulsar is not visible in amateur telescopes, but the nebula (discovered in 1731) shows up as a tiny oval disk 6 × 4 arcminutes in dimension. Look for M1 between the horns of Taurus, and use high magnification. It is about 6,300 light years distant, 10 light years in diameter (it continues to expand at the rate of 1,100 miles per second), and 1,000 times the luminosity of our sun. Because of its importance in understanding the death of stars, the Crab Nebula is one of the most intensely studied objects in the sky.

TRIANGULUM—the Triangle (tri-ang-you-lum)
(chart 2)

Spiral Galaxy M33: The second brightest galaxy in the northern sky is barely bright enough to see with the naked eye but is an easy target for binoculars. Located 15 degrees southeast of the famous Andromeda Galaxy M31, M33 is slightly farther (a little over 3,000,000 light years). In contrast to M31, which is 12 degrees from being oriented edge-on, M33 is essentially face-on; they appear entirely different in binoculars and telescopes of all sizes. M33, with its loose, open structure (and consequently very low surface brightness), appears as a haze of light several times larger than the moon. A very large amateur scope, however, shows its spiral structure as well as the clouds of hydrogen gas within it (the brightest cloud, NGC 604, is 12 arcminutes northeast of the galaxy's center). Look for M33 in the northern part of Triangulum, four-tenths of the way from Alpha Trianguli to Beta Andromedae.

URSA MAJOR—the Great Bear (ur-sa may-jer)
(charts 1 and 4)

Double Star Mizar: Perhaps the most famous double star in the sky, Mizar (also known as Zeta Ursae Majoris) is the second star from the end of the handle of the Big Dipper; it is the easiest double star to find. Mizar's 4th-magnitude companion, Alcor, is 708 arcseconds (12 arcminutes) from Mizar, and the two are easily visible unaided to people with better than average eyesight. Alcor is 14 light years beyond Mizar and not in orbit around it, but the two stars may feel the pull of each other's gravity and are traveling on parallel paths through space. That Mizar itself is a double star was discovered in 1650; it was the first double star known. This duo's magnitudes are 2.2 and 3.9, and they are separated by 14 arcseconds. At a distance from Earth of 78 light years, their true separation is at least 33 billion miles, or 10 times the distance from Pluto to the sun. The brightest of Mizar's two stars is about 50 times the luminosity of the sun. All three stars are white.

Planetary Nebula M97: Known as the Owl Nebula, this planetary is very near the bowl of the Big Dipper. It is large and dim; at 11th magnitude, it is one of the faintest objects listed in this book. A large amateur telescope with high magnification shows the two dark patches that are the Owl's "eyes." Its apparent diameter is 3 arcminutes. The Owl is about 1,300 light years distant and about a light year across.

Spiral Galaxies M81 and **M82**: These two famous galaxies, which lie ⅔ degree apart in the northern part of Ursa Major, are always associated with each other. In fact, they form a contrasting pair: M81 is a large, bright 7th-magnitude nearly face-on spiral with an oval shape; M82 is smaller, fainter (magnitude 8.5, but with a higher surface brightness than its neighbor) cigar-shaped irregular galaxy. At one time M82 was thought to have suffered a major explosion; now its contorted shape is considered the product of a

Spiral Galaxy M81. Photo by Jack Schmidling.

recent (astronomically speaking) close encounter with M81 and consequent tidal interactions. The two are about 12 million light years distant and are at the center of the small Ursa Major Group of galaxies.

Spiral Galaxy M101: Lying 6 degrees due east of Mizar, this face-on spiral, though a magnitude 7, has a low surface brightness because of its enormous size. In a small telescope, it appears as an unimpressive glow surrounding a bright nucleus; a large telescope reveals luminous clouds in its spiral arms. It lies about 25 million light years distant. Its nickname is the Pinwheel Galaxy.

URSA MINOR—the Small Bear (ur-sa my-ner)
(chart 1)

Double Star Polaris: The North Star is actually two. Look for the main star's 8.2-magnitude companion 18 arcseconds distant. Polaris is a giant star approximately 300 light years from Earth. This is one double star that is visible every clear night.

VIRGO—the Virgin or Young Maiden (ver-go)
(charts 4 and 8)

Sky gazers with good telescopes can see several faint galaxies in Virgo, Leo, and Coma Berenices. These galaxies are members of a huge massing called the Coma-Virgo Cluster (or often just the Virgo Cluster). Studying this cluster of 2,000 galaxies some 60 million light years distant is critical to establishing the size and age of the universe, and the Hubble Space Telescope is often turned toward it. Almost two dozen galaxies can be seen in small telescopes, of which the brightest are described here. Our own Milky Way appears to lie on the very outer edge of the Coma-Virgo Cluster.

Elliptical Galaxy M49: At magnitude 8.5, this giant elliptical is one of the largest galaxies of all, with a diameter nearly twice that of our Milky Way and containing five times more stars. Like the other galaxies of the cluster, it is 60 million light years distant.

Elliptical Galaxy M60: Another giant elliptical, M60 is a 9th-magnitude featureless object. The 11th-magnitude elliptical galaxy M59 is ½ degree to the west.

Elliptical Galaxies M84 and M86: These giant elliptical galaxies (both 9th magnitude) lie a mere ¼ degree apart near the center of the Virgo Cluster, with several fainter galaxies nearby. It has been suggested that M86 is a foreground object, but it is more likely a member of the cluster; it is actually quite close to M84 and surrounding galaxies.

Elliptical Galaxy M87: M87, the largest galaxy in the cluster, lies near its center. One of the largest galaxies known, it may have 30 times as many stars as our Milky Way. It looks like an 8th-magnitude splotch! Photographs reveal a jet of material shooting out of its side and thousands of globular clusters surrounding it.

"Sombrero Galaxy" M104: In contrast to the other bright galaxies in Virgo, which are elliptical, the Sombrero is a nearly edge-on giant spiral. Its name derives from both the dark dust lane that nearly bisects it and the big, bright area at its center that gives it its distinctive shape. Its dust lane is among the most easily visible outside the Milky Way. The 8th-magnitude Sombrero is several times larger and 10 times more luminous than our Milky Way. It lies on the far side of the Virgo Cluster.

VULPECULA—the Fox (vul-peck-you-la)
(chart 5)

"Dumbbell Nebula" M27: By far the brightest planetary nebula, this 6.5-magnitude cloud is easily visible in binoculars and small telescopes. A showpiece of the summer sky, it was the first planetary nebula discovered (by Messier in 1764). Its name derives from its bilobed shape, which resembles a weight lifter's dumbbell. Find it by first locating Sagitta the Arrow; the Dumbbell is 3⅓ degrees due north of the star at the Arrow's tip. (The 8th-magnitude globular star cluster M71 is in the same binocular field of view.) The Dumbbell is 8×4 arcminutes in size (about 2 light years) and about 1,000 light years distant. It has about 100 times the luminosity of our sun. Use medium and high magnifications to bring out its odd shape.

✴

Chapter Twelve

OBSERVING THE MILKY WAY

T he largest and grandest structure in the entire sky cannot be seen from most people's homes. The Milky Way appears only if the sky is dark, so city dwellers are out of luck. Many people see it best while on vacation in sparsely populated areas.

The Milky Way is our inside-out view of our own galaxy—a system of hundreds of billions of stars moving together through space. Our galaxy has the shape of a flat spiral, and we live away from its center. All the stars in the sky (including our sun) are in the Milky Way galaxy. Those relatively nearby are the bright stars that form the constellations. The countless others, too distant and too dim to see individually, make up the hazy backdrop of the Milky Way.

The Milky Way appears as a band of light that wraps around the sky. At first glance it might seem to be composed of a gaseous material, but even the smallest telescope shows it to consist of, in Galileo's words, "innumerable stars . . . quite beyond calculation." Although individually faint, the stars are so numerous that their luminosity blends to form a continuous band of pale light. The total number of stars in the Milky Way is an astounding several hundred billion—a believable number if you look through a telescope on a truly dark night. It's amazing to realize that each star is like our sun and that many have a family of planets (and some of those planets may be inhabited). A sublime pleasure is to silently cruise the Milky Way with binoculars or a low-power wide-angle telescope and absorb the beauty and implications of what passes into view.

The Milky Way encircles the earth at an odd, canted angle. One branch is overhead in summer and another in winter, while during the spring, the Milky Way lies near the

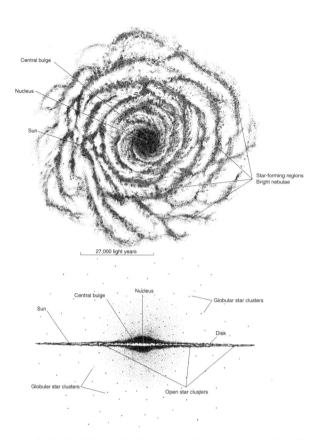

The Milky Way is a flattened spiral with a thick and bright center. Most of the stars (including the sun) lie in a narrow disk of stars about 1,000 light years wide and 130,000 light years across. A bulge several thousand light years in diameter surrounds the center, while a faint halo of stars surrounds all.

horizon. Early in the evening in late summer it dominates the sky, but at certain times (early evening in late spring) it lies flat along the horizon and can't be seen at all. Although it bisects the sky, it is not symmetrical. At first glance, it might seem as if we were at its center, but closer inspection shows that it is considerably brighter and wider toward Sagittarius and Scorpius than in the opposite direction, toward Orion. The implication—that we are off center—is correct, but there's a twist. The truth is that the Milky Way is not equally intense in all directions; it is much brighter in *its* center than elsewhere. That center lies in Sagittarius. The Milky Way is brighter toward this direction not because we are closer to the center (we are not), but because there are so very many more stars there.

Generations of astronomers have labored to unravel the structure of the Milky Way. We now understand it well enough to be able to visualize our position within it. So let's tour it, beginning at the center.

The center lies about 27,000 light years from Earth, in the direction of Sagittarius. Find the "teapot" that outlines Sagittarius on a dark summer evening; the Milky Way's center is above and to the west of the "spout." There is nothing special for us to see at this point because countless clouds of gas block our view—although because radio waves pass through clouds, radio astronomers are able to determine what is there.

Notice that the Milky Way's center is surrounded by an elliptical bulge of billions of stars, several thousand light years in extent. Most of it, too, is hidden from view, although a part known as the Great Sagittarius Star Cloud peeks above the plane of the galaxy; using binoculars, look for a very bright concentration of the Milky Way near the stars Gamma and Delta Sagittarii. The Star Cloud, too distant to see the individual stars within it, looks like a smooth glowing patch of light. This is as close to the center of our Milky Way as we can see with our eyes. (See "Sagittarius.")

The bulk of the Milky Way is a flat disk of stars not much more than 1,000 light years in breadth and over 100,000 light years in extent. Stars (and especially gas) are not distributed uniformly throughout the disk; instead, they are concentrated in spiral arms that wrap around its center. These arms are separated by several thousand light years, and few bright stars lie between them. Evidence suggests that the arms radiate from the ends of a starfilled rod, or bar—called the "Milky Way Bar"—which slashes through the center of the Milky Way, indicating we live in a barred spiral galaxy.

A short distance away we see part of the spiral arm closest to the galaxy's center. This arm is almost completely obscured by clouds of gas, though a section is visible as a small bright "cloud" northeast of the star Mu Sagittarii. Known as the Small Sagittarius Star Cloud, it is a lovely sight in binoculars on a dark summer night.

The next spiral arm outward from the center is the Sagittarius Arm. It lies about 6,000 light years from Earth and extends from Carina, below the southern horizon, through Sagittarius, to terminate in Scutum. This arm encompasses all the glorious objects in the summer Milky Way so beloved by amateur astronomers, including lustrous nebulae and star clusters. Many are bright enough to see in good binoculars, making the Sagittarius Arm a happy hunting ground during summer star parties.

The farthest extent of the Sagittarius Arm is marked by the Scutum Star Cloud, near the star Alpha Scuti. This is actually where the Sagittarius Arm curves away from us, and it appears bright because we are looking down its length. North of this dense area of the Milky Way (easily visible in binoculars) is a gap between the Sagittarius Arm and the next arm outward; that gap lies in Aquila.

Sagittarius and Scorpius from Joshua Tree National Park, California. Trees in foreground are blurred as the camera tracks the rotating sky. Photograph by Bruce Gottlieb.

Our sun lies on the inner edge of the Orion Arm, which wraps entirely around the sky. From Aquila northward through the section of the sky near Cassiopeia and Perseus in the summer and through Orion and Monoceros in the winter, we are looking at the Orion Arm. The part of the Orion Arm closest to us lies in the (surprise!) direction of Orion, about 2,000 light years away. The famous Orion Nebula is near the arm's center, as are many of our nearby star clusters and nebulae. So many more bright stars lie in or near Orion than in any other part of the sky because that is the direction of our closest spiral arm. The Orion Arm, however, is thinner than the Sagittarius Arm—and it looks it.

The section of the Orion Arm richest in stars and star clusters is in Cygnus. The most ample part is the Cygnus Star Cloud, near Gamma Cygni. When we face Cygnus, we are looking down the length of our own arm (astronomically speaking!), which curves away and beyond and on around the Sagittarius Arm.

Notice that the Milky Way is split—divided into two parallel streams by the Great Rift. The Great Rift consists of giant clouds of dark gas and dust that block light from the stars beyond. The rift extends from a point south of the star Deneb to below the southern horizon. One of the most obvious features in the nighttime sky, it is well worth exploring with binoculars or a telescope. In some places, the edge of the rift is surprisingly sharp.

At least one additional spiral arm lies beyond Orion. Little of it is visible, but a gap in the Orion Arm in Cassiopeia and Perseus lets us glimpse the Perseus Arm, which lies 7,000 or so light years from Earth. The famous Perseus Double Cluster (see "Perseus") is a pair of star clusters, barely visible to the naked eye, which lies within the Perseus Spiral Arm. Beyond the Perseus Arm we see only a few faint star clusters.

The galaxy is rotating, carrying our solar system with it toward Cygnus; face Cygnus in the summer sky and you are facing the direction of its rotation. Keep in mind that our solar system takes about 230 million years to complete one circuit of the Milky Way.

At one time it was thought that the Milky Way was the entire universe. When in the 20th century other galaxies were found to exist, they were called "island universes." Truly the many other galaxies visible through a telescope help us understand our own.

STAR CHARTS

Chart 5

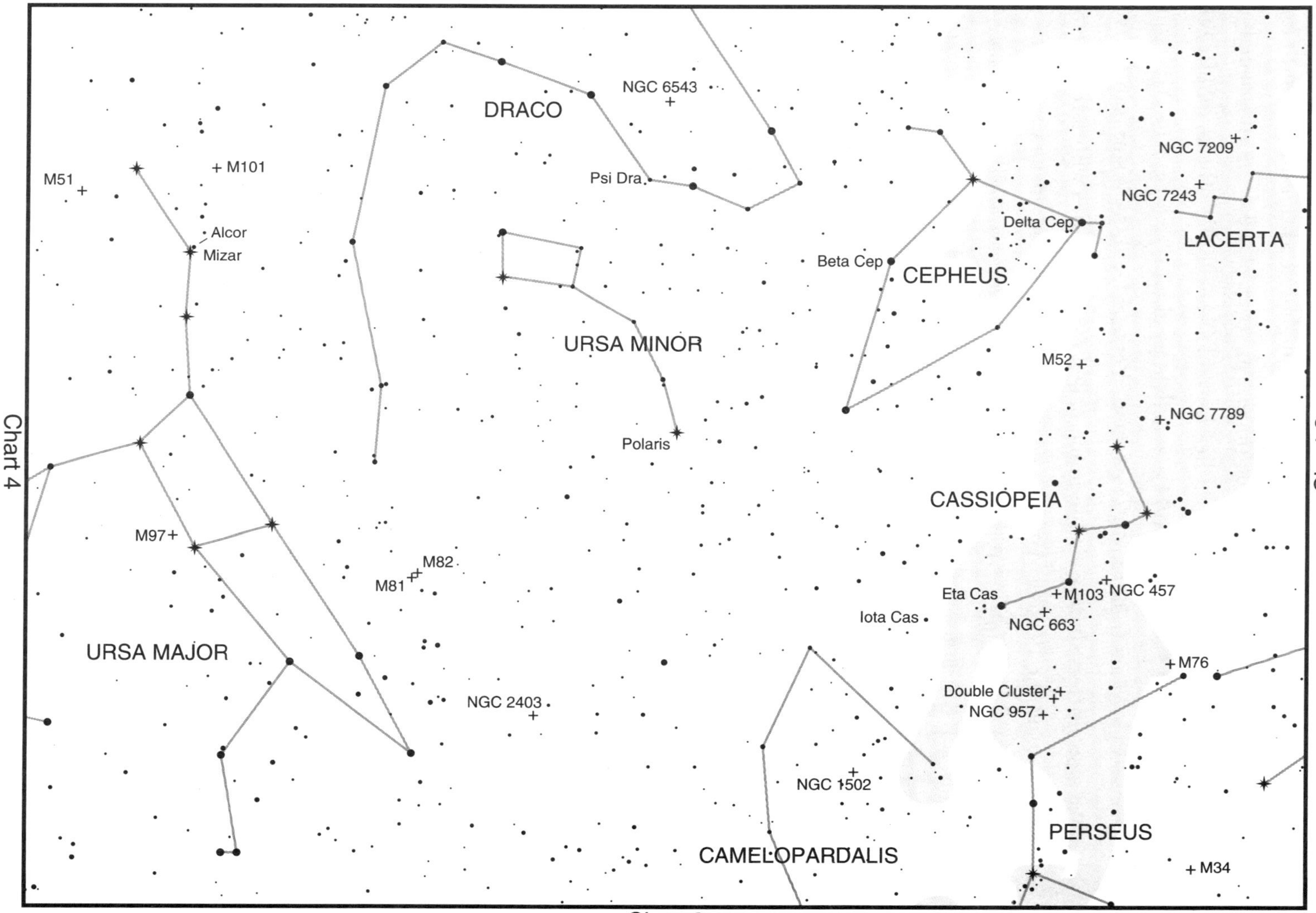

Chart 4

Chart 2

Chart 3

Chart 1

LACERTA

NGC 7209

NGC 7243

NGC 7789

M52

Delta Cep

CEPHEUS

Beta Cep

CASSIOPEIA

Eta Cas

M103 NGC 457

NGC 663

Iota Cas

M76

Double Cluster

NGC 957

PERSEUS

M34

CAMELOPARDALIS

NGC 1502

NGC 6543

Psi Dra.

DRACO

URSA MINOR

Polaris

NGC 2403

M82

M81

M101

Alcor

Mizar

M97

URSA MAJOR

M51

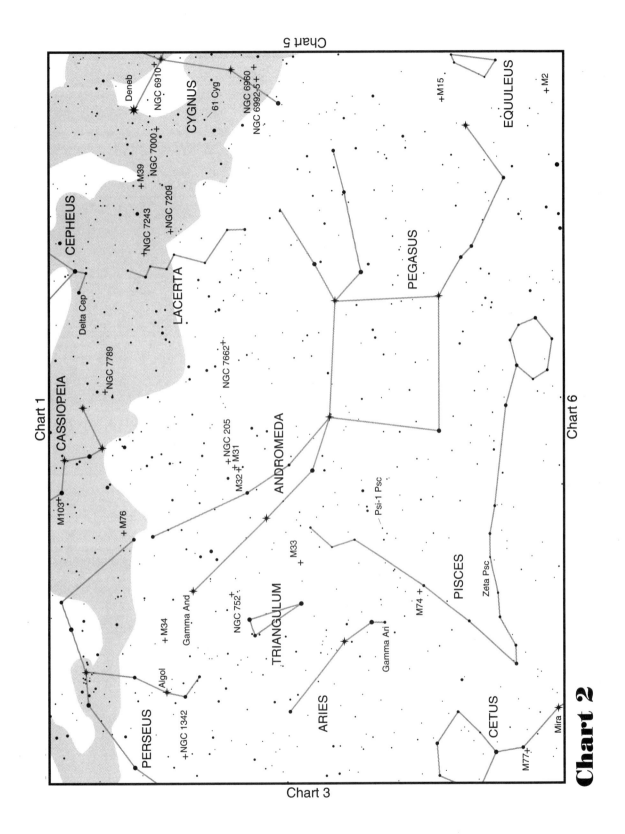

Chart 1

Chart 5

Chart 3

Chart 6

CASSIOPEIA

CEPHEUS

Delta Cep

M103 +

+ NGC 7789

+ M76

Deneb

NGC 6910 +

+ M39

NGC 7000 +

61 Cyg

NGC 6960

NGC 6992-5 +

CYGNUS

+ NGC 7243

+ NGC 7209

LACERTA

NGC 7662 +

ANDROMEDA

+ NGC 205

M32 + + M31

PEGASUS

EQUULEUS

+ M15

+ M2

PERSEUS

Algol

+ NGC 1342

+ M34

Gamma And

NGC 752 +

TRIANGULUM

M33 +

ARIES

Gamma Ari

Psi-1 Psc

M74 +

PISCES

Zeta Psc

CETUS

M77 +

Mira

Chart 2

Chart 2

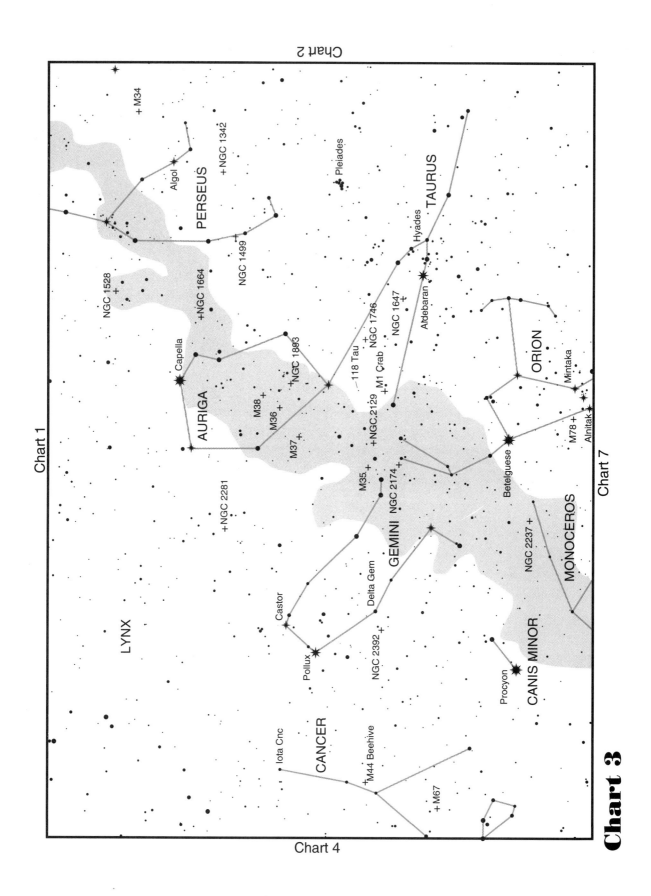

Chart 1

Chart 4

Chart 7

Chart 3

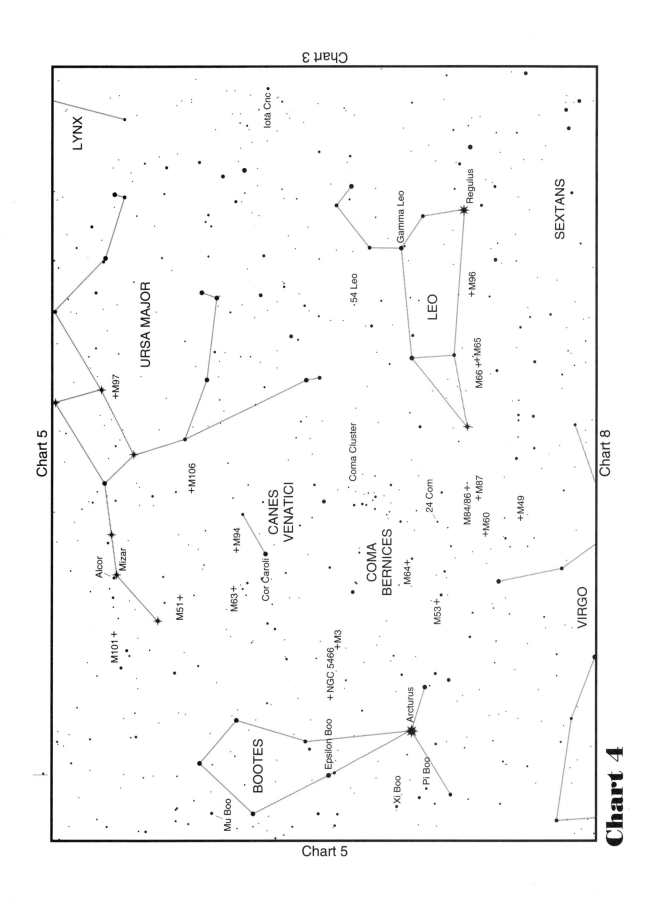

Chart 3

LYNX

URSA MAJOR

Iota Cnc

Gamma Leo

Regulus

54 Leo

+M96

LEO

SEXTANS

M66 +·+M65

Chart 5

+M97

+M106

CANES
VENATICI

Coma Cluster

Alcor

Mizar

+M94

M63+

Cor Caroli

COMA
BERNICES

24 Com

M84/86 +·
+M87

+M60

+M49

Chart 8

M51+

M64+

M101 +

M53 +

VIRGO

+ NGC 5466

+M3

BOOTES

Epsilon Boo

Arcturus

Mu Boo

Xi Boo

Pi Boo

Chart 5

Chart 4

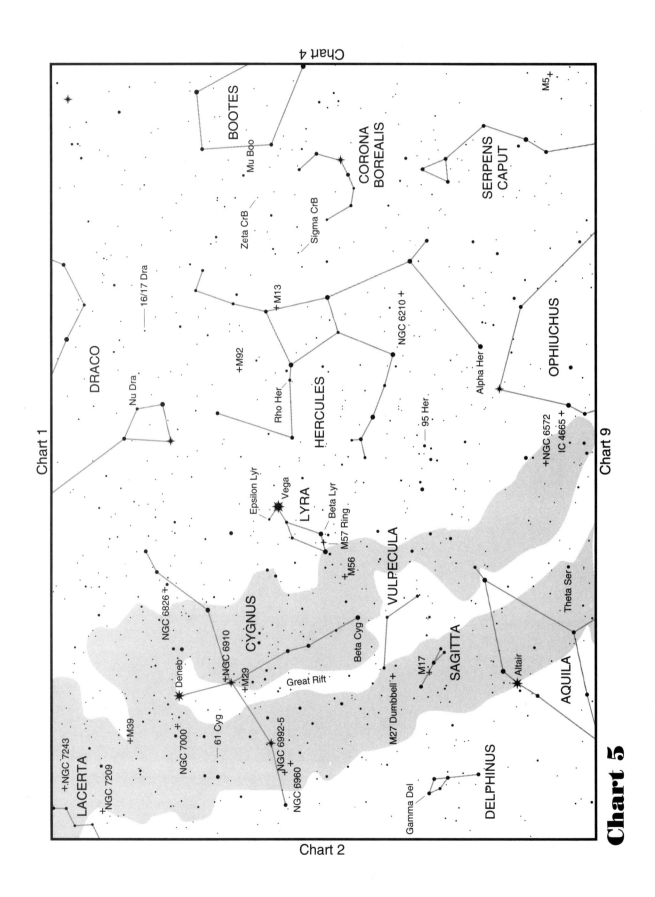

Chart 4

Chart 1

Chart 2

Chart 9

BOOTES

Mu Boo

CORONA
BOREALIS

Zeta CrB

Sigma CrB

SERPENS
CAPUT

M5 +

16/17 Dra

M13 +

NGC 6210 +

DRACO

+M92

Nu Dra

Rho Her

HERCULES

95 Her

OPHIUCHUS

Alpha Her

+NGC 6572

IC 4665 +

Epsilon Lyr

Vega

LYRA

Beta Lyr

M57 Ring +

+M56

+NGC 6826

CYGNUS

VULPECULA

+NGC 6910

Beta Cyg

+Deneb

+M29

Great Rift

M17
+

M27 Dumbbell +

SAGITTA

Theta Ser

+M39

NGC 7000 +

61 Cyg

+NGC 6992-5

Altair

AQUILA

+NGC 7243

LACERTA

+NGC 7209

+NGC 6960

Gamma Del

DELPHINUS

Chart 5

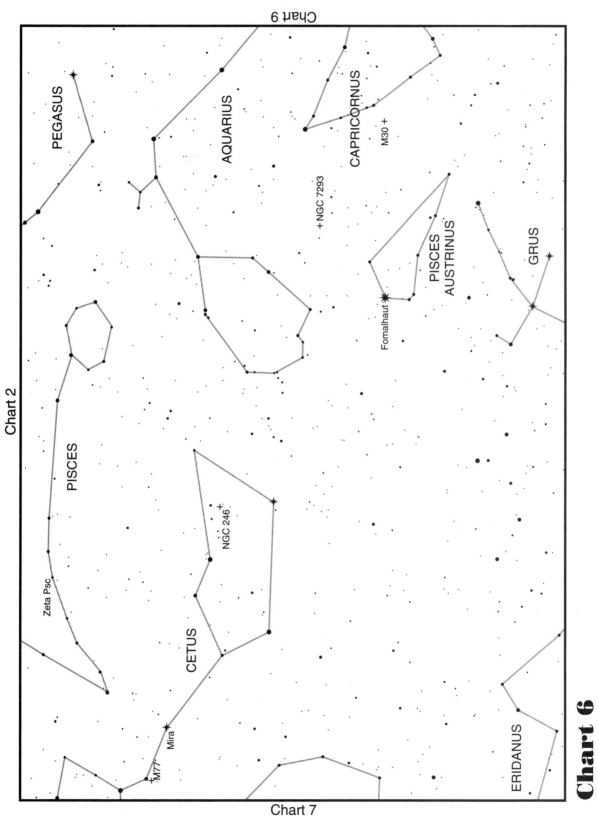

Chart 9

Chart 2

PEGASUS

AQUARIUS

CAPRICORNUS

M30 +

+ NGC 7293

PISCES AUSTRINUS

Fomalhaut

GRUS

PISCES

Zeta Psc

CETUS

NGC 246 +

Mira

+ M77

ERIDANUS

Chart 7

Chart 6

Chart 6

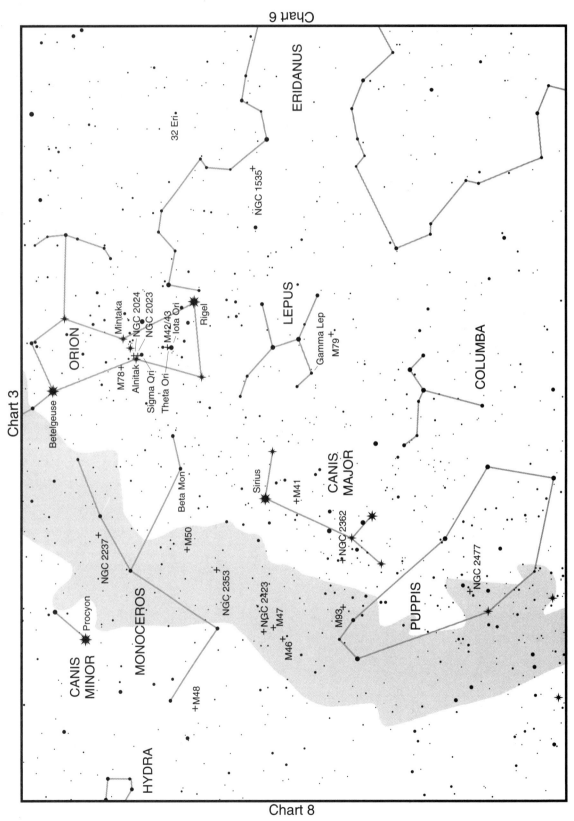

Chart 3

ERIDANUS

32 Eri

NGC 1535

LEPUS

Gamma Lep
M79

ORION

Mintaka
NGC 2024
NGC 2023
M42/43
Iota Ori
Rigel

M78
Alnitak
Sigma Ori
Theta Ori

Betelgeuse

COLUMBA

Sirius

CANIS
MAJOR

M41

NGC 2362

Beta Mon

CANIS
MINOR

Procyon

MONOCEROS

NGC 2237

NGC 2353

M50

NGC 2423
M47

M46

M93

PUPPIS

NGC 2477

M48

HYDRA

Chart 8

Chart 7

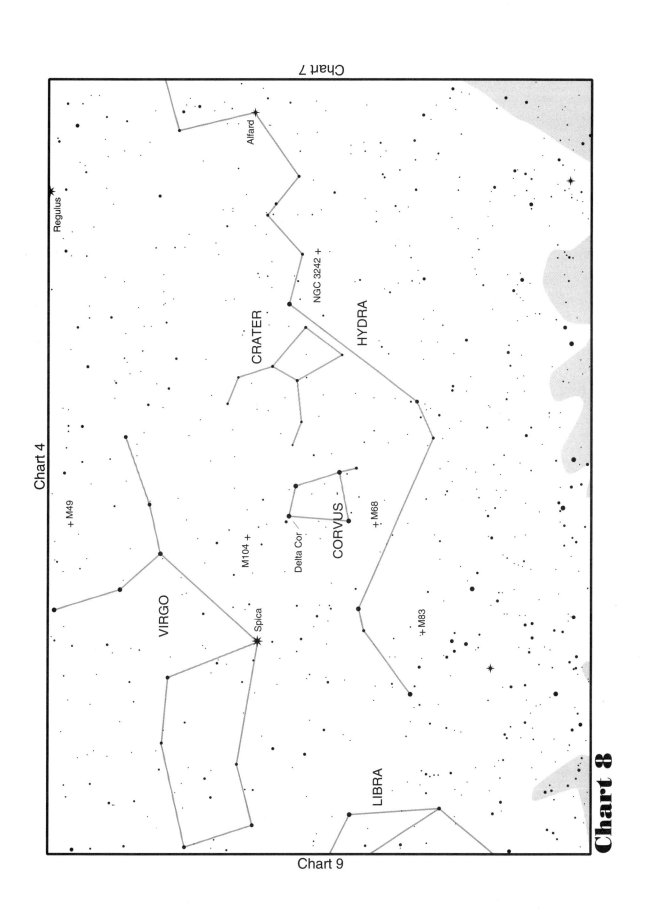

Chart 7

Chart 4

Regulus

Alfard

CRATER

NGC 3242 +

HYDRA

+ M49

M104 +

Delta Cor

CORVUS

+ M68

VIRGO

Spica

+ M83

LIBRA

Chart 9

Chart 8

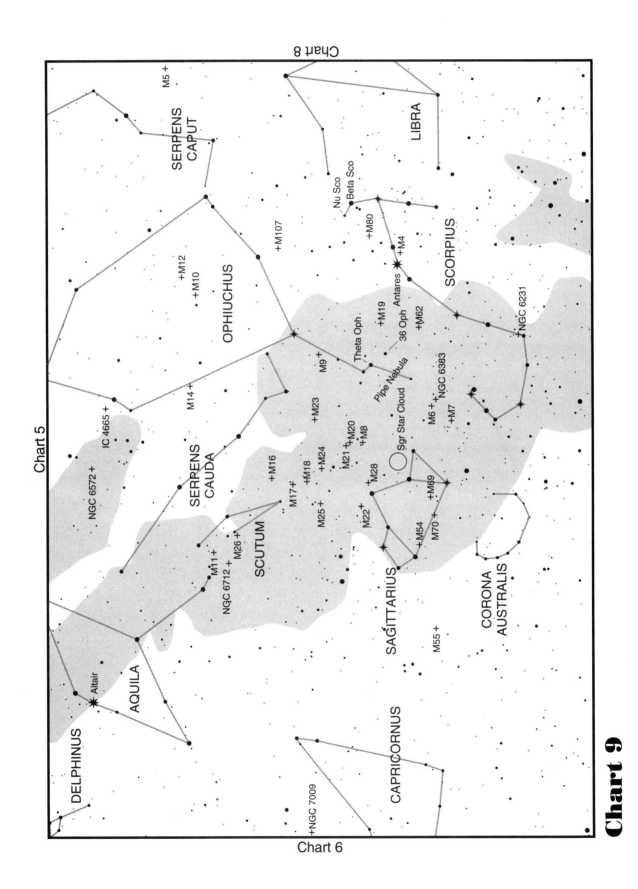

Chart 8

Chart 5

Chart 6

SERPENS CAPUT

M5 +

LIBRA

Nu Sco
Beta Sco

+M80

+M107

+M4

+M12
+M10

Antares
36 Oph

SCORPIUS

OPHIUCHUS

Theta Oph

+M19

+M62

NGC 6231

M9 +

+NGC 6383

M14 +

+M23

Sgr Star Cloud

M6 +
+M7

Pipe Nebula

IC 4665 +

+M20
+M8

M21 +

SERPENS
CAUDA

+M16

+M24

+M18

NGC 6572 +

M17 +

+M28

M25 +

+M69

SCUTUM

+M22

M70

M11 +
M26 +

SAGITTARIUS

+M54

NGC 6712 +

CORONA
AUSTRALIS

Altair

AQUILA

M55 +

DELPHINUS

CAPRICORNUS

+NGC 7009

Chart 9

Chapter Thirteen

✦

WHERE TO GO FROM HERE

This book is a starting point, but where do you go to learn more? Begin at your local **planetarium**. Planetariums are community resource centers for astronomical matters. They exist to help people learn about the stars, and the staff will be happy to answer your questions and to recommend books and telescopes. An astronomy museum and book store may be on site. If there's no planetarium in your town, look for one in a nearby city.

There is simply no better way to learn about something than by hanging out with people who are knowledgeable and enthusiastic. A local **astronomy club** can be an invaluable source for personal recommendations on equipment and also a source of used telescopes. Astronomy clubs conduct regular "star parties," where the members gather to view the sky through a variety of telescopes. Your local planetarium or science museum will know about astronomy clubs in your area, and a comprehensive list is posted at the *Sky & Telescope* magazine's Web site at http://www.skypub.com.

Two excellent monthly **astronomy magazines** are *Astronomy* (1027 N. Seventh St., Milwaukee, WI 53233) and *Sky & Telescope* (Sky Publishing Corp., P.O. Box 9111, Belmont, MA 02178-9111). *Astronomy,* which claims to be the more colorful of the two, is aimed at armchair astronomers. *Sky & Telescope* has a long reputation of excellence in interpreting astronomy. Both carry advertisements for astronomy items, including telescopes, and both publish annual guides to planetariums, astronomy clubs, and equipment vendors.

Travelers need maps and guide books, especially when they are in unfamiliar territory, and sky gazers are no exception. A good **star atlas** is a valuable companion to this book. Many atlases are available, from simple sets of charts that show only the stars you'll see with your unaided eye to heavy (and expensive) multiple-volume atlases, works of cartographic art that show all the faint objects visible in a large amateur telescope. The most complete star atlases now come on CD-ROM and run on desktop computers. Basic star atlases are described on page 91. To purchase an atlas, check the advertisements in *Astronomy* and *Sky & Telescope*. The most comprehensive source for observing aids is Willmann-Bell, Inc., P.O. Box 35025, Richmond, VA 23235 (write for a catalog).

Observing guides describe the hundreds or even thousands of objects plotted on star atlases. Most are lengthy tables of numbers. It is not very romantic to extract data from tables, but if you want to know the fundamental characteristics of an object, they can be found in the many observing guides that are available. The most descriptive is the three-volume *Burnham's Celestial Handbook*. Its 2,138 pages leave little unsaid about thousands of stars and deep-space objects, and it is filled with interesting information. Also popular are the *Cambridge Guide to the Stars and Planets* and *Star-Hopping for Backyard Astronomers*. These books and more are available from the vendors mentioned above.

If you have a personal computer, explore the sky with the many **astronomy computer programs** available for DOS, Windows, and Mac operating systems. Programs show the positions of the stars and planets at any time, the constellations in great detail, and simulated eclipses and the motions of the planets. Some programs provide detailed digital maps of the sky, showing everything visible through the largest telescope you will ever own. Armchair astronomers can find picture collections on CD-ROM to browse and games with astronomical themes to play, plus educational software intended for school use. More good astronomy software exists than a person could use, and the problem is to know which are the better programs. Check monthly reviews in *Astronomy* and *Sky & Telescope* magazines for recommendations. Lists of available software are posted on the World Wide Web at the Astronomy Software Revue site at http://www.skypub.com/software/mosley.html and Planetarium Software at http://www.seds.org/billa/astrosoftware.html.

Finally, there is a universe of astronomy information available on the **World Wide Web**—even on cloudy nights when you cannot see the stars. You'll discover a seemingly limitless supply of news, facts, research, graphics, and even software. Good places to start are Sky Online at http://www.skypub.com and the *Astronomy* magazine Website at http://www.kalmbach.com/astro/astronomy.html. Links to all these places and more can be found at the Griffith Observatory's Website at http://www.GriffithObs.org. In addition, your local planetarium or science museum undoubtedly has a Website that would provide a good starting point.

INDEX